THIRTY YEARS OF
SOUTH AFRICAN
SOCCER

Managing Editor
Thami Mazwai

Contributing Authors
S'Busiso Mseleku • Sy Lerman • Billy Cooper • Thomas Kwenaite
Raymond Nxumalo • Bongi Sishi • Bafana Shezi • Matshelane Mamabolo
Bareng-Batho Kortjas • Pule Mokhine • Sello Rabothata
Matshelane Mamabolo • Linda Rulashe

*MultiChoice Africa is proud to have made possible 'Thirty Years
of South African Soccer'. The book represents, in a small way,
our contribution to our country and the 2010 bid.*

THIRTY YEARS OF
SOUTH AFRICAN
SOCCER

MAFUBE
PUBLISHING (PTY) LTD

FOREWORD BY THE MINISTER OF SPORT AND RECREATION, NGCONDE BALFOUR, MP

Sport in South Africa has been an important tool in the struggle for political change. It formed a part of the vulnerable underbelly of a repressive regime that regarded international participation as an exclusive right of white South Africans.

At the same time, sport was used by successive colonial and apartheid regimes as an ideological instrument to entrench white domination and stifle black advancement.

By deliberate design, the documentation of South African sporting history had been limited to white sport, creating the false impression that black South Africans had no interest in sport. Those regimes and their supporters reckoned without the resilience of their black compatriots. They never understood or ignored (to their ultimate detriment) the depth of the passion of black South Africans for sport, particularly, the beautiful game – soccer.

Despite their oppression, black South Africans embraced football as their own. A natural flair for the game was evident from as early as the 19th century when football was first played here. This book is a timely reminder that football is the sport of the people of our country. No government, no matter how repressive, could take this away from those who lived for the game. Not even the denial of resources and access to facilities could blunt the passion that our people feel for the game.

The unfolding history of South African soccer is well chronicled in *Thirty Years of South African Soccer* that should be compulsory reading for any serious follower of the game. It provides valuable insights into the struggles that soccer encountered on its journey to become the most popular and widely-supported sport in the country, and indeed, the world.

It explodes the myth that white people held the monopoly on sport in this country. They might have controlled the resources but they had no control over the natural affinity that the majority of our people had for football. From very early days, football was dominant and administered in every corner of our country. Associations blossomed. Legends strode across our playing fields. Their followers worshipped the very grounds where they stepped on and strutted their magical skills. Quite often, football was a temporary escape from the oppression that South Africans suffered in their daily lives. It was the one activity that not even Apartheid legislation could deny the people.

Football has experienced many highlights over more than a century of the game. Sadly, there were also tragedies along the way. This book is an attempt to give expression to the untold stories of those who have contributed towards the growth of football and its popular appeal.

There is no denying that football experienced its own brand of racism. It is also true that numerous attempts, albeit misguided at times, were made to bring all soccer lovers together under one umbrella. It was only with the dawning of a political democracy that soccer succeeded in its initiatives to form a single controlling body for the sport.

The game is now on a new horizon and still retains its popularity as the leading sport in the country. This book is, by far, not the final chapter on the beautiful game. It is, however, an invaluable resource that lays the groundwork for documenting the personal stories of the unheralded soccer heroes of our country.

BMN BALFOUR, MP
MINISTER OF SPORT AND RECREATION
October 2002

PUBLISHER'S ACKNOWLEDGEMENTS

It is indeed a fitting tribute to South African soccer that a phalanx of some of our outstanding soccer scribes have contributed to what is certainly a definitive chronology of the evolution of the game in our country.

My brief from sponsors of the book, MultiChoice Africa and representative Nolo Letele, the CEO, and his right hand man, Lebogang Hashatse, the General Manager for Corporate Affairs, was to have it ready for the 2002 World Cup. It was envisaged that every fan would want the book as part of his or her paraphernalia to back Bafana Bafana. Alas, it was not to be as we missed the deadline by a mile. The reason was simple – we had to dig and dig to produce some of the most original copy available on South African soccer. Indeed, as you go through these pages you will realise that this is not simply a casual collection of soccer stories, but a series of deeply felt accounts of the triumphs, and the passion that went into them, that characterised the rise of our soccer to what it is today.

The next World Cup will see a South African squad that is much improved, beyond even the dynamic one that invaded Japan and Korea just a few months ago. As it is now halfway to the next World Cup, the hope is that this book will spur Danny Jordaan and Irvin Khoza and their bid team to bring the 2010 World Cup to this land of miracles. Minister of Sports Ngconde Balfour, who embraced the project from its inception and hence his opening message, shares this view.

This book fills a big void as very little has been written about the history of our soccer, even though it is the country's national sport, and I say this advisedly. National sports are not determined by the politics of wealth and power, but by the sheer, magnetic ability of the men in the field to touch the hearts of millions of ordinary South Africans, to produce in them one of two powerful emotions – joy and sorrow. No other game can claim to ignite the nation's passions as soccer does. And the Beautiful Game is just as commanding in the rest of Africa, perhaps even more so because some national communities do not have a second sporting code to compete for the people's devotion. It is soccer all the way, and this could explain why countries such as Nigeria have produced such formidable national teams, why the depth of talent runs so deep.

Our battery of writers is an enthusiastic lot, drawn from most of the country's newspapers. These include *Sowetan*, and at one time its predecessors the *World* and *Post* newspapers, which have for many years been the bibles of black soccer. In fact, there was a time when no Press conference on black soccer could be held if there was no reporter from the *Sowetan*. Later on *City Press* joined *Sowetan* as the homes of black football and millions of South Africans religiously followed the game from the pages of these newspapers.

We also have contributors from the other national newspapers. Phil Nyamane was brought in as adviser, and we had the benefit of both his expertise and his memories, which span several decades of exciting football – in fact from the days (specifically 1972) when he was my deputy sports editor at the banned *World*. He then worked for a daily publication, writing about soccer and boxing, before retiring.

The indefatigable Sbu Mseleku paints an evocative picture, in Chapter 2, of the early days of soccer and its first stars. In Chapter 1 Sello Rabothata describes Bafana's illustrious performance at the last World Cup. He should know best: he was in the technical team in Korea and Japan. Linda Rulashe, one of our blossoming women sports writers, provides two developmental pieces on AmaGlug-Glug and Banyana Banyana. But the story of South African soccer is not all glory of course – we also touch on some of its sadder occasions. Other contributors added substantially to the story. Each of these writers has provided original insights into the game as it progressed over the years.

I have no doubt that you will enjoy reading this book, and that you will let it be your companion as we journey to Germany in 2006 to ensure the boys bring it home this time.

THAMI MAZWAI
PUBLISHER

First published in 2003 by
Mafube Publishing (Pty) Ltd

ISBN 0 624 04107 7

2 4 6 8 10 9 7 5 3 1

Packaged for Mafube Publishing by
Sunbird Publishing (Pty) Ltd

SUNBIRD
PUBLISHING

34 Sunset Avenue, Llandudno,
Cape Town, South Africa

Registration number: 4850177827

PACKAGER Dick Wilkins
EDITOR Peter Joyce
DESIGNER Peter Bosman
PICTURE RESEARCH Farieda Classen
PROOFREADER Nazli Jacobs
PRODUCTION Andrew de Kock

REPRODUCTION BY
Unifoto (Pty) Ltd, Cape Town

PRINTED AND BOUND BY
Fishwicks, Durban

In conjunction with

FRONT COVER *Main photograph: South African football icon Jomo Sono in joyful mood. Photo strip, left to right: Kaizer Motaung heads the ball; Nelson Mandela cheers as Bafana captain Neil Tovey raises the African Cup of Nations; John Moshoeu rounds an opponent; early stars "Ace" Mgedeza and Patrick Ntsoelengoe in action; Lucas Radebe wrestles the ball away from England's Trevor Sinclair in a 2003 friendly.*

BACK COVER *A young Kaizer Motaung (front row, third from left) and his Select X1, a squad which eventually became Kaizer Chiefs.*

TITLE *The Slovenian 'keeper saves in his team's World Cup match against South Africa.*

ABOVE *Bafana's Aaron Mokoena beats Slovenia's Pavin in the air.*

OPPOSITE, TOP TO BOTTOM *Siyabonga Nomvete celebrates after scoring South Africa's first goal against Slovenia; Chiefs and Pirates fans in happy pose; President Thabo Mbeki with sports minister Ngconde Balfour and, on the right, Urs Kneubuhler from Switzerland. The occasion: a media briefing during South Africa's World Cup 2006 bid process.*

CONTENTS

CHAPTER 1

WORLD CUP 2002

Bafana Bafana's progess to soccer's premier event placed them among the very best of footballing nations. It was a magnificent achievement — especially as, until quite recently, they had been banned from the international scene.

MOST SOUTH AFRICANS were (and many still are) delirious with happiness that the national side put up such a gallant display in the 2002 World Cup, soccer's premier event. After all, even before going to South Korea and quite apart from the matches themselves, Bafana Bafana had achieved a memorable triumph simply by qualifying for the finals – an achievement that automatically puts you right up there among the world's best soccer nations.

Bafana were very much aware of this. Indeed, so optimistic, even confident and certainly hyped up was the squad that the failure to reach the second round of the finals came as a real shock, and there was deep consternation in their camp – not least because the they had been eliminated on a technicality. Bafana lost out on a paper-thin goal difference – they scored five and conceded as many goals while Paraguay, then group rivals for advancement to the next stage, netted and conceded six.

Unsure of the reception waiting for them at home, the boys composed a dirge-like song that revealed their trepidation. And defender Cyril "Skhokho" Nzama led them in the singing: "Sizo'ngena kanjani emakhaya, so'ngena kanjani! S'khokhele Sono, siy'emakhaya; thina so'ngena kanjani!" (which means, in rough translation, "How will we get into our homes, how will we get in! Lead us home Jomo Sono! How will we get in!).

But to their pleasant surprise they "got in" easily enough. In fact they were given a heroes' welcome, by a big crowd, on their arrival at the Johannesburg International Airport on June 14.

And to top it all they were invited to the homes of President Thabo Mbeki and former president Nelson Mandela!

OPPOSITE *Star defender Lucas Radebe celebrates after scoring South Africa's second goal against Spain at the Daejean World Cup Stadium, on June 12, 2002. Bafana had twice come back from behind, but a 56th-minute blunder by goalkeeper Arendse let in Spain's third, and decisive, goal.*

GETTING TOGETHER

Although Bafana failed to reach the second stage of the World Cup, the technical team could not be faulted in their groundwork for the big occasion. The squad went into camp from May 6, 2002, in the upmarket, picturesque, sun-sand-and-sea resort town of Umhlanga Rocks north of central Durban on the KwaZulu-Natal coast. The South African Football Association (Safa) booked the boys into the exclusive Beverley Hills hotel for the time it would take to prepare them – and to select of the 23 players who would represent the country at the greatest single sporting event in the world.

Ten of the 33 soccer stars present at Umhlanga Rocks would have to be dropped. The tension was palpable as players and technical staff wondered to themselves, and perhaps among themselves in quiet corners, just who faced the axe. Everyone was trying to impress, giving his superhuman best at the training sessions.

Then the axe fell. The players were given two days' break during which Sono announced the touring squad for South Korea. Those who had been chosen bade sad good-byes to the unlucky ten who had not made the cut.

On May 17 the squad regrouped at a smart hotel near Johannesburg International airport for final preparations for the big event. It was only on their arrival here that the truth – that the biggest challenge of their lives was almost upon them – struck the players between the eyes,

Before leaving for overseas, Bafana were addressed by deputy president Jacob Zuma, and Minister of Sports Ngconde Balfour, at a farewell dinner. The gist of the speeches was that the players were the country's ambassadors and their conduct, both on and off the field, would reflect on South Africa and its people.

Safa's vice-president, Irvin "The Iron Duke" Khoza, echoed the same sentiments when addressing his colleagues and the squad both in Durban and Johannesburg.

Some had been part of the not-too-successful France '98 World Cup effort, among them assistant coach Trott Moloto and players

Lucas Radebe (captain), Quinton Fortune, Benni McCarthy and Hans Vonk, masseur Joe Ramokadi, security personnel Eric Soshibo and Ali Hlongwane, and Safa executive members David Nhlabathi and Reuben Mahlalela, Safa's second vice president.

STARTING OFF WITH A BANG

Just before the finals, Bafana created high expectations from even the most cynical of their fans by winning the Reunification Cup tournament in Hong Kong, where they set up camp for two weeks (actually "camp" is perhaps not quite the right word; they stayed at the comfortable Royal Garden hotel and trained at the splendid Mong Kok stadium). They began by eliminating Scotland 2-0 (goals by Teboho Mokoena and George Koumantarakis) and, two days later – following a second-half brace by Benni McCarthy – chalked up a convincing and historic victory over Turkey in the final.

In the tunnel leading to the ground, Bafana's singing had compelled a curious Turkey coach, Senol Gunes, to ask Sono what the singing was all about. "It's a war song," the SA coach quipped. Ninety minutes later Bafana triumphantly lifted the Reunification Cup.

The tournament had proved a huge morale-boosting tune-up for the World Cup proper. Bafana capped their victorious pre-Cup run by flying to Japan and Ueno City, near Kobe, rolled out the red carpet for them before they beat the locals, Vissel Kobe (3-1) on May 26.

The squad's routines in Japan, in one of the world's most crowded cities, revolved around the training sessions, the team meetings – and the shopping expeditions.

Head coach Matsilele Jomo Sono, his assistants Trott Moloto and Khabo Zondo, and goalkeeper coach Farouk Abrahams, devoted serious time to studying tapes, discussing tactics and planning each forthcoming first-round game. Some of Bafana's overseas-based players contributed valuable insights and background material on what they knew about the footballing skills of their scheduled opponents.

On its arrival in South Korea for their World Cup campaign, the squad were met at Seoul Airport by the South African ambassador, Sydney Khubeka, and given a tumultuous welcome by the locals.

Their successful Reunification Cup was safely behind them. But memories of the tournament remained both sharp and gratifying, because it marked their first-ever victory over European opposition.

THE FINAL BATTLES

Bafana were based in Gangneung City, where a special training ground had been erected for them at the Riverside pitch. Gangneung is a seaside city of about 240 000 people in the north-eastern part of South Korea. It's a tranquil area, known for the beauty of its scenery and its sunrises, for its heritage from a long and colourful past – and for the splendid seafood served by its myriad restaurants.

The squad's dedication and focus impressed those who watched them; everybody knew that this last-minute preparation was vital for success. And the friendly spirit of both the players and the technical staff made it a pleasure for the

BELOW *Bafana-Bafana stood tall after winning the warm-up Reunification trophy in Hong Kong, defeating both Scotland and Turkey in the process. A happy Benni McCarthy holds the cup aloft.*

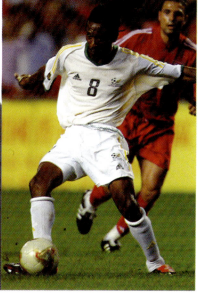

ABOVE *South Africa's McDonald Mukanzi shields the ball from Scotland's James McFadden in the first Reunification match, played in Hong Kong in May 2002. South Africa won 2-0.*

LEFT *Thabo Mngomeni plays the ball through the Turkish midfield in the second Reunification encounter.*

FAR LEFT *Jabu Pule receives a wise word of advice from President Thabo Mbeki before he and his Bafana teammates head off to World Cup 2002.*

horde of foreign journalists who had homed in on Gangneung, though good public relations remained a relatively minor part of what was now a very serious business. In fact, contact with anyone outside Bafana's closed circle was discouraged: reports from South Africa that somehow filtered into camp tended to have the players reflecting negatively on their chances, and they became restless with worry. They were ordered not to read newspapers or 'phone home.

In the event though, Bafana managed to perform well, always with honour and sometimes with outstanding distinction.

Their dramatic second half comeback against Paraguay, in the opening game at the Busan Asiad main stadium, on June 2, is generally regarded as one of the highlights of the round-robin stage of the World Cup. After being 2-0 down, and getting a dressing down from Sono at the interval, they came out for the second half spitting fire and drew level from Teboho Mokoena's strike and Quinton Fortune's spot-kick.

Happy with that performance, and with positive vibes coming from South Africa, Bafana

ABOVE *Victory smiles – MacBeth Sibaya embraces Siyabonga Nomvete after his second-half goal against Slovenia.*
LEFT *One of the more dramatic moments in Bafana's first-ever World Cup finals win – Lucas Radebe climbs high to beat Slovenia's Ales Ceh in the air.*

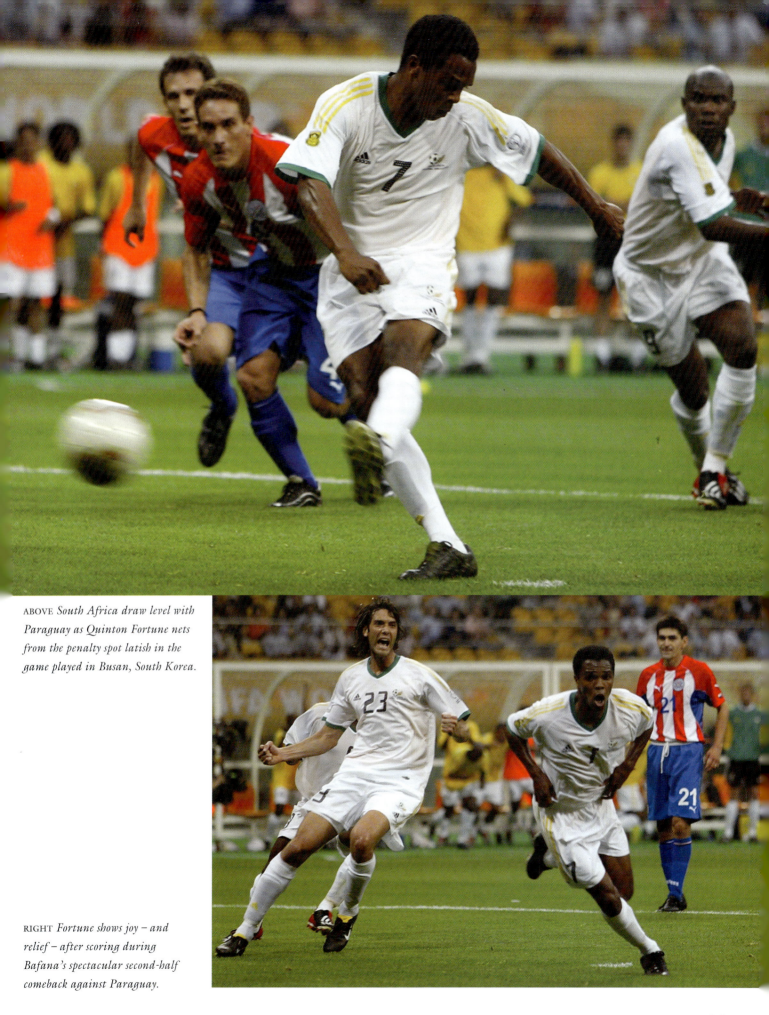

ABOVE *South Africa draw level with Paraguay as Quinton Fortune nets from the penalty spot latish in the game played in Busan, South Korea.*

RIGHT *Fortune shows joy – and relief – after scoring during Bafana's spectacular second-half comeback against Paraguay.*

ABOVE *Bafana lost narrowly to Spain, one of the giants of world soccer, in the third and crucial Group B match. Here Siyabonga Nomvete battles with Spain's Xavi for control of the ball.*

looked forward to the next game, against Slovenia, with optimism.

The South Africans made history at the Daegu stadium on June 8 when Siyabonga Nomvete scored – the only goal of the game – to give Bafana their first victory in the finals of a World Cup. Nomvete had in fact failed to connect a header, but the ball deflected from his right knee and nestled in the net. But who was complaining! Sono was on cloud nine and indeed, so

were all of us as the second round now seemed within reach.

Bafana now needed a draw against Spain at the Daejeon stadium on June 12 to reach the second round – and, with their self-confidence boosted and their spirits high, they believed they could do it.

But that was not to be. After coming back twice to level matters, a lapse of concentration from the defence saw Spain sneaking in a late goal to take the game 3-2.

South Africa's hopes now rested on the match between Slovenia and Paraguay, and on comparative goal averages. Then news began filtering through and even these hopes were dashed: Paraguay's two-goal triumph (final score 3-1) broke our hearts. It was the end for Bafana.

There was some suspicion that forces had been at play in Paraguay's victory, a suspicion fueled by the fact that Slovenia were leading 1-0 at the interval, and that Paraguay were reduced to ten men for the better part of the second half. But this was speculation; nothing could be proved, and in the end the only thing that mattered was the scoreboard.

But still, the national team had by no means disgraced South Africa; indeed they could be proud of what they had accomplished, and they were received back as heroes. A week after their arrival, they were invited to Parliament and given another rousing welcome. They were overwhelmed by the receptions.

Not too long afterwards new coach Ephraim "Shakes" Mashaba and his knowledgeable assistant, Styles Phumo, took over the reins.

With these appointments, and with the players' encouraging efforts in the World Cup behind them, Bafana Bafana is bound to blossom in the coming years.

ABOVE *New coach "Shakes" Mashaba and his assistant Styles Phumo.*

World Cup 2002

Hosts: South Korea and Japan

QUALIFYING ROUNDS: *Final standings*

	PLAYED	WON	DRAWN	LOST	FOR	AGAINST	POINTS
South Africa	6	5	1	0	10	3	16
Zimbabwe	6	4	0	2	7	5	12
Burkina Faso	6	1	2	3	7	8	5
Malawi	6	0	1	5	4	12	1

FINALS: *Group B match reports*

Bafana Bafana 2 – Paraguay 2. June 2. Venue: Busan. Attendance 40 000. Bafana goals: Tebeho Mokoena (64; deflected off Paraguay's Struway), Quinton Fortune (90). Paraguay goals: Santa Cruz (39), Arce (55). Paraguay were the more effective team in attack, despite fielding just one forward in Santa Cruz, although they reduced their chances by deciding to retain their two-goal lead by defending in depth. All credit, however, to the South Africans for coming back from that deficit.

Bafana Bafana 1 – Slovenia 0. June 8. Venue: Daegu. Attendance: 47 226. Bafana goal: Siyanbonga Nomvete (4). A somewhat substandard game. The Slovenians were guilty of poor marking, their morale low after a disastrous week in which they had seen their star player dismissed from the camp and coach Sreko Katanec banished to the stands for persistently arguing with the referee. The South Africans showed impressive pace on the break.

Bafana Bafana 2 – Spain 3. June 12. Venue: Daejeon. Attendance: 31 024. Bafana goals: Benedict McCarthy (31), Lucas Radebe (53). Spain goals: Raul (4), Mendieta (45), Raul (56). The narrow result sent the South Africans crashing out of the World Cup. Showing good pace and plenty of spirit against their more fancied opponents, they had twice come back from behind, but the 56th minute goal by Raul, following a blunder by keeper Arendse, proved too much of a challenge, and Paraguay's victory over Slovenia in the other Group 3 match sealed their fate.

KEY PLAYERS

Lucas Radebe Once again Radebe came off a long lay-off from injury to lead Bafana, this time on the most important campaign of all. And he scored one of the better goals.

MacBeth Sibaya Many thought that coach Jomo Sono was promoting his own club players, but Sibaya proved to be one of the tournament's best midfielders. It came as no surprise when he was promptly offered an overseas contract.

Siyabonga Nomvete Showed that he had grown in stature while playing for Udinese in the Italian Serie A. His running off the ball was a marvel to watch, and he also scored a crucial goal.

CHAPTER 2

THE EARLY DAYS

Soccer was introduced to South Africa by British settlers more than 120 years ago. By 1912 they had passed some of their skills, and all of their love for the game, to the country's black people.

FOOTBALL IN SOUTH AFRICA goes back to the late 19th century, when British settlers brought the game to the country. The first-ever recognised club was Pietermaritzburg County, formed in 1879 and, at first, forced to play against military selections since there was very little opposition among the region's residents.

But more clubs were born, and in 1882 the Natal Football Association was formed. Pietermaritzburg County could now test their mettle against such teams as Umngeni Stars, Durban Alpha and Natal Wasps. And, even though County was the oldest club, Wasps soon came to dominate the league, winning the championship four years in succession (1883 to 1886). Among other Natal clubs that soon made their appearance were Ramblers, Berea, Swifts, Savages, Pirates, 24th Regiment, 64th Regiment, Victoria Athletics and Victoria County.

In 1887, a knockout competition was played and, according to early records that have survived, Victoria Athletics beat Ramblers 1-0 in the final and, after lifting the trophy, went on to maintain a stranglehold on the competition until Savages of Pietermaritzburg ended their winning streak in 1891. During this period, there was also strong rivalry between Durban and Pietermaritzburg clubs. Representative matches between the two towns were played each year. And, as in club competition, Durban dominated the derbies, winning 2-1 in 1883, 2-0 in 1884 and 2-1 in 1886. The best that Pietermaritzburg could do was two goalless draws, in the 1885 and 1887 versions of the tournament.

While all this was happening, there were moves to start organised soccer in other areas. A certain Mr A. Dickson, a former Queens

Park Rangers player, tried to establish the game in Port Elizabeth but his efforts failed to bear any fruit. Then in 1890 two Englishmen, Messrs B. Warburton and J.H. Weaver, founded Pioneers FC in Cape Town, the Mother City. Their initial idea was to challenge the dominance of British military teams – which they did, and in the process soon became a force to be reckoned with.

Other clubs quickly followed, a proliferation that led to the formation, in the following year, of the Western Province Football Association, a body based at the Green Point track just west of the city centre but which later moved its headquarters to the Hartleyvale stadium. From here they set up a league and a knockout competition known and remembered as the O'Reilly Cup.

From these humble beginnings emerged the Football Association of South Africa (FASA) which became soccer's countrywide controlling body. It should be noted, however, that this was the colonial era – all the clubs and associations mentioned were exclusively for white members, and for white spectators.

BIRTH OF BLACK FOOTBALL

According to records, the first club for black South Africans was Bush Bucks, formed way back in 1912 by the Reverend Carlton, a missionary based at the Ifafa Mission on the Natal South Coast. The club had no local opposition and had to travel to the Adams College – a trip that took them two days on foot! – to play against the school soccer team.

A decade and a half later, in 1928, Solomon Gabriel Senoane, who had just joined Johannesburg municipality and was appointed director of "native recreation", began organising the game for the miners and other black residents of the highveld townships, efforts that led to the formation of the Johannesburg Bantu Football Association in 1929. Senoane received valuable help in his initiatives from Graham Ballenden, manager of the municipal "Native

ABOVE *The great soccer pioneer Steve "Kalamazoo" Mokone was the first black South African to campaign overseas.*
OPPOSITE *Vusi "Stadig My Kind" Makhathini played in the Zuka-Baloyi Cup, the closest thing to national representation in the early years.*

Affairs" department, and from the American Board missionary Dr Ray Phillips.

Ballenden and Phillips were great believers in using organised sport to reinforce social control. Phillips said his main objective was to "place football amongst the Natives on a sound footing and to eliminate gambling and other objectionable practices".

The committee of the early Johannesburg Bantu Football Association (JBFA) was: president – I.H. Radebe; vice-president – S.P. Mqanduli; secretary S.G. Senoane; patron and advisor G. Ballenden; honorary president A.W. Oliver; honorary vice-president L.I. Venables; recording secretary A.K. Nobanda. Among Senaone's first tasks was to approach the city council with a view to transferring control all those football grounds set aside for "natives". The association used the Wemmer Sports Grounds for its matches until April 1931, when the Bantu Sports Grounds in Von Weilligh Street were inaugurated.

The JBFA was the cornerstone of organised football among South Africa's blacks, the foundation on which were built the associations such as the Transvaal Bantu Football Association, South African Bantu Football Association, the South African National Football Association and eventually the present South African Football Association (Safa).

During the same year the JBFA was formed, other Africans, elsewhere, came together to organise the Beautiful Game. Notable among the pioneers was the Pietermaritzburg Bantu Football Association, with its affiliated Washbank association. Together, the two comprised the Natal Bantu Football Association. Pietermaritzburg, obviously, was the headquarters of both associations. A number of clubs, from as far afield as Johannesburg, travelled down to play friendly matches.

Another powerful association was the Durban and District Bantu Football Association, popularly known as the "D and D", which grew and flourished under the leadership of the visionary Henry Posselt Ngwenya.

The name Ngwenya is mentioned in the same breath as Senoane, Bethuel Morolo, Job Rathebe and Dan Twala – all pathfinders in the development of the game. Ngwenya's association was the first to undertake long-distance team trips to and matches against neighbouring countries, among them Botswana (then known as Bechuanaland), Zimbabwe (formerly Southern Rhodesia) and the Congo. He won the admiration of all when he acquired a bus for his association; he also invested in fixed properties in Inanda. The D & D squad was the first to be coached by a white man, a certain Topper Brown.

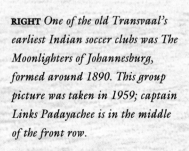

RIGHT *One of the old Transvaal's earliest Indian soccer clubs was The Moonlighters of Johannesburg, formed around 1890. This group picture was taken in 1959; captain Links Padayachee is in the middle of the front row.*

SHIFTING LOYALTIES

However, infighting, the scourge of South African football, unhappily impacted on the development of the game. It led to, among other things, the departure of Dan Twala and a group of clubs away from the JBFA to form the Johannesburg African Football Association.

The "official" reasons given for the split are flimsy, and they were undoubtedly more concerned with internal politics than with sport. The "Bantu" in JBFA was seen as a negative tag: all the organisations that used Bantu as part of their names were felt to be pandering to the Native Affairs Departments of the different white-controlled municipalities.

Other reasons given related to education – Twala felt unable to serve under someone with far less formal schooling than he had – and to tribalism. The feeling was that "we cannot be led by a Mosotho" – a reference to Senoane. Hence most of the clubs that moved with Twala were predominantly Nguni speaking. Twala's group used the Bantu Sports Ground, where he was an administrator, and the Senoane group played at the Wemmer Sports Grounds.

Nor was Natal spared the infighting. African Wanderers were expelled from the Durban and District Football Association for misconduct and joined the Pietermaritzburg Bantu Football Association. And so it went on all the way up to and during the 1950s – loyalties, links and liaisons were subject to constant and bewildering change. In 1959, the South African Football Association suspended T.A. Nene, secretary of the Natal African Football Association – a move which led to D & D severing its ties with the Natal African Football Association in favour of membership of the Natal Bantu Football Association. It was in 1959, too, that Durban and District Bantu Football Association itself split, to give birth to the Durban and County Bantu Football Association.

Perhaps the boldest move of the time – of an era notorious for its racial exclusion and repression – was the 1959 agreement between the Football Association of South Africa (FASA) and the South African Bantu Football Association (SABFA) to create the basis on which non-racial soccer would be played in the future. Among those at the crucial meeting were Frederick William Fell, chairman of FASA; his colleagues David Snaier and Syd Kimber; Mr Bethuel

ABOVE *The boss – Dan Twala founded the Johannesburg African Football Association.*

RIGHT *Ethnic soccer – "Africans" against "Coloureds" in the 1950s.*

Morolo and, representing the SABFA, Harry Madibane and Johannes Sibiya.

It is interesting to note that Fell had been a founder member of the Confederation of African Football (CAF) in 1956. However, South Africa had been kicked out of the inaugural African Cup of Nations, held in Egypt in the following year, for insisting on sending an all-white soccer team.

Eventually – in January 1962 – an agreement was reached between FASA and SABFA in terms of which the African body accepted associate member status within FASA. The document that was signed later included the South African Coloured and South African Indian football associations. The move led to the formation of the Inter-Race Soccer Board.

THE COMPETITIVE FIFTIES

Meanwhile, a lot had been happening on the actual playing fields as well as in the boardrooms. Much earlier, in 1953, a soccer match between the South African "Africans" and the South African Coloured Association was played at Johannesburg's Wembley stadium. The "Coloureds" led 3-0 at half-time but the blacks came back well in the second half and the match ended in a 3-all tie.

One of the more popular competitions of the time was the Zuka-Baloyi Cup, which was contested by clubs from the then Transvaal, Eastern Transvaal, Northern Transvaal, Natal, Free State, Griqualand West and Basutoland (now Lesotho). Playing in these tournaments was the closest thing to national representation.

Some of the prominent teams of the time included the Highlanders, Jack Hammers, Blue Bells, Bergville Lions, Ladysmith Home Boys, Old Natalians, Kroonstad Shamrocks, Try Again, Durban Wanderers, Bush Bucks, Moonlight Darkies, Moroka Lions, Linare and Bantu FC. The latter two still play in the Lesotho Premier League.

It was in these competitions that men such as Dr Stephen "Kalamazoo" Mokone, Grant Khomo, Stadig "My Kind" Makhathini, Petros Senzeni Zulu, Sydney "Buya" Msuthu Nkutha, Barbar T. Maphalala, Willard "Windoda" Msomi and Gibson "Danger" Maketelele, to mention just a few, shone like stars.

BELOW *Steven "Kalamazoo" Mokone shows off his ball skills. The road to non-racial soccer would be long and hard.*

CHAPTER 3

CHAMPIONS OF MIXED SOCCER

For years a regiment of good men battled to free soccer from its racial chains, and for years their efforts were sabotaged by FASA, South Africa's "official" representative body.

RIGHT *Tough talk – officials of the SA Soccer Federation, led by Rama Reddy (second from right) meet the African National Congress's Steve Tshwete (right) and Thabo Mbeki (third from right) in Lusaka, November 1988. Other delegates include Vincent Baartjies, Alex Abercrombie and Merriman Zuma. South Africa's future political leaders made it clear to the competing soccer bosses that there would be no international recognition for local football until there was complete sporting unity.*

THE APARTHEID YEARS – the best and the worst of times. Times of unrelenting repression, punctuated by harassment, bannings, and untold misery.

Through it all, the South African Soccer Federation (SASF), its officials and its fans – who sustained unwavering loyalty and total commitment to the cause of non-racial football in the struggle for justice, equality and dignity – made the best of those worst times. Courageous leaders such as Dan Twala, Norman Middleton, S.K. Chetty, Danny Naidoo, R.K. Naidoo, Ashwin Trikamjee, George Singh, and Abdul Bhamjee carried the flag during apartheid's most repressive period. Attorney Singh was banned and hounded by apartheid's

agents. Middleton, Bhamjee and others were refused passports to travel overseas.

Officials of the South African Council on Sport (SACOS), the umbrella body for all non-racial sporting bodies in the country, were the special victims of the vicious, racist minority regime of the time. Hassan Howa, Frank van der Horst, Manickum N. Pather, Reggie Feldman, who were leaders of some of the sporting codes, were treated like common criminals. Other luminaries, among them Dennis Brutus and Sam Ramsamy, were forced into exile to pursue the struggle for non-racism in sport through the South African Non-Racial Olympic Committee (Sanroc).

THE STAB IN THE BACK

The South African Soccer Federation survived in spite of the onslaught. Household names such as Eric "Scara" Sono, Kaizer Motaung, Percy "Chippa" Moloi, Difference "City Council" Mbanya, Dharam Mohan, Bernard "Dancing Shoes" Hartze, Rashid Khan, Hans Moses, Ralph Hendricks, Links Padayachee drew large crowds to the matches in which they appeared.

From its very inception in 1951 – that is, before the country itself was represented at Fifa – the Federation was constituted as a national non-racial body. After its launch it communicated with the then Southern Africa Football Association – later renamed the Football Association of South Africa (FASA) – with a view to forming one national controlling body to represent all footballers "irrespective of race, colour or creed". But FASA was playing a double game. Even while it was communicating with the Federation, it secretly applied for Fifa membership. Its application was accepted at the Fifa congress held in Helsinki in 1952.

FASA's action was a blatant stab in the back of the Federation which, in the years that followed, struggled for recognition by Fifa. Neither was it able to get FASA to join hands to form one national body.

Fifa was aware FASA did not comply with the provisions of its statutes, that it violated Article 2, which covers discrimination against country or individuals and requires national associations to foster friendly relations among players by encouraging football at all levels. But, still, the world body ignored the non-racial Federation's application for recognition.

FASA did its best to keep South African sport racially divided. It embarked on a policy of divide and rule, and pressured government and the municipalities to bar non-racial sports bodies

ABOVE LEFT *An airborne Kaizer Motaung (in a Chiefs' shirt). Motaung became an icon of the game.*
BELOW *Rewards – South African Soccer Federation officials are all smiles after clinching a sponsorship deal.*

from using public fields and stadiums. It used its financial resources to keep other non-white soccer bodies – the splinter South African Bantu Football Association (SABFA, later to be called the South African National Football Association, or SANFA), the so-called SA Coloured Football Association (SACFA) and the SA Indian Football Association (SAIFA) – from joining the Federation. FASA's purpose was to hoodwink Fifa into believing it linked all the country's "ethnic groups". But the plain fact that there was no mixed soccer at club level simply exposed the dishonesty of the whole exercise.

The world was later shocked to learn that blacks were barred from attending FASA matches at many grounds and stadiums – even as spectators.

In 1964, Fifa suspended and subsequently expelled FASA for practicing racial discrimination, and for its representation of minority whites only. The suspension did not stop racial discrimination. Instead, much later (in 1973), FASA tried to circumvent the ruling by introducing a one-off "multi-national" tournament. Participating teams were selected on the basis of race. Fifa disapproved of such "international" matches as they enflamed racial animosity. And indeed they did create racial hostility, even riots, as witnessed during the second-leg inter-club Chevrolet "Champion of Champions" final between Kaizer Chiefs and Hellenic at the Rand Stadium in 1975 (see page 28).

In his own inimitable way, poet Don Mattera, at one of the Transvaal Soccer Board's functions, rendered his version of what the Protea – South Africa's national flower, ironically also the emblem on the Bafana Bafana jersey – really meant for the voiceless, voteless, downtrodden people of our country.

He said the flower depicted the fall of the racial white establishment and was symbolic of the bond between all those struggling to be free.

ABOVE *Signs of the times: a visit to Johannesburg's Apartheid Museum reveals just how racially regimented the soccer scene – indeed the whole of South African society – was until good men began to come together in the late 1970s. Picture shows one of the museum's workers flanked by a display of colour-based identity books.*

ABOVE *South African football was well on its way to full integration by the early 1980s. Here Orlando Pirates' Phillip Setshedi leaps past a prone Richard Kellet of Wits University as Andy Karajinski (3) looks on. The first multi-racial NPSL soccer league had been launched in 1978 – and won, ironically, by the all-Portuguese Lusitano club.*

ABOVE *Norman Middleton takes notes – his South African Soccer Federation opposed all forms of racial football in the country.*

CHAPTER 4

BREACHING THE BARRIERS OF RACE

The first chinks in the massive armour of sporting apartheid appeared in the early Seventies, when a "national White X1" played against a "national Black X1". Although the players and spectators were segregated, it was hailed as a major breakthrough.

A 40 000 CROWD, about half of them black and half of them white, huddle in pouring rain under a sea of umbrellas at the Rand stadium. The blacks sit on one side of the pitch, the whites on the other. They are watching two soccer teams, who are similarly segregated.

Stupid and short-sighted as the wider world of the early 1970s viewed this strange occasion, on which a so-called national White XI played a national Black XI, South Africans of that time hailed it as a major breakthrough in the granite-like wall of apartheid.

Ironically, this misguided and naive way of edging away from grand Verwoerdian apartheid dealt South Africa soccer a blow from which it has yet to recover, or at least to fully rectify, almost 30 years later. Instead of easing tension and creating a measure of racial harmony, the segregation of the spectators and teams in what was dubbed "multi-national" competition (in order not to antagonise a rabid right wing section of the population) tended only to encourage suspicion and strife.

And, to make matters worse, the high expectations of blacks at the Rand stadium on that stormy, bizarre but still historic night – that their skilled ball-juggling team would succeed in taking apart the more dour and less spectacular whites – was cruelly shattered. The black team suffered a 3-0 beating. What is more, the most revered of black South African soccer heroes were on show, while the white team was made up of little-heralded amateurs playing in what was then an all-white, mainly professional National Football League, and they were far from the best representatives of their footballing community.

The whites were better tutored, more experienced and more adept in such elementary tactics as using the offside game, and they took ample advantage of players who had suffered the lonely deprivations of an out-of-touch ghetto existence. When it came to the subleties of the game, the blacks were novices.

These misguided early efforts at easing apartheid were a tragedy for South African soccer, because white players, white officials and white spectators were not drawn into the partnerships so vital for development, and the growth of the game was stunted. Nevertheless, the "multi-national" concept served a significant purpose in that it marked the beginning of the end of segregated soccer in South Africa.

PROGRESS AGAINST THE ODDS

Up to 1970 soccer in South Africa, at all levels, was (officially) played by all-white or all-black sides. And, to erect the racial barriers still higher, white teams played only against white teams and black teams only against black teams.

Ninety out of a hundred spectators at white professional matches in the National Football League were white; blacks were herded into a small section of the grounds in what were often conditions of extreme discomfort. Black games were watched only by blacks.

Nevertheless both "white soccer" and "black soccer" were followed enthusiastically, and, in practice (in many instances) blacks supported both black and white soccer and had their favourite teams in each of the two spheres.

OPPOSITE *Soccer in South Africa remained strictly segregated until the 1970s. Here, Pirates' Alfred "Ace" Mgedeza (left) and Chiefs' Patrick "Ace" Ntsoelengoe compete for the ball at a packed Orlando Stadium. The "white" soccer world was long denied the skill and flair of stars such as these.*

ABOVE *Brazilian Walter da Silva, a leading member of the Highlands Park squad that raised soccer standards throughout the country.*

BELOW *Kaizer Chiefs battle it out with Lusitano in August 1978. Genuine multi-racial soccer had been introduced the previous year but, unhappily for the game, not on a partnership basis – the white-controlled bodies virtually surrendered to their black counterparts.*

Moreover, such was the Nationalist government's obsession with race that cross-cultural sporting contacts with other "non-whites" rarely took place: officialdom discouraged even Africans, Indians and "Coloureds" from playing together. The only multi-racial arena, in which various non-whites and a handful of whites mixed, was a so-called South African Soccer League.

Almost entirely excluded from international competition because of apartheid, soccer in South Africa had lagged behind European and South American countries in introducing professionalism. But the professional era was finally launched in 1960 and flourished through the growing popularity of teams like Highlands Park, Durban City, Durban United, Cape Town City and Hellenic, on the one (white) side, and Orlando Pirates, Moroka Swallows and Cape Town Spurs on the other .

Highlands Park, in particular, with its rare mixture of South African-born whites, Brazilians, Scots, Englishmen, Portuguese and players from what was then Rhodesia, raised the standard in the country to a new level with stars like Jorge Santoro, Walter da Silva , Bobby

Hume, Willie McIntosh, Charlie Gough, John Stewart, George Ryder, Joe Frickleton, Vasco Pegado, Freddie Kalk, Malcolm Rufus and Stan Jacobitz thrilling the crowds. And then there was all-white Durban City, probably the most popular club in the country in the 1960s although, ironically, close to 70 percent of their following was of Indian origin.

TROUBLED TRANSITION

All this began to unravel in the 1970s – after the introduction of "multi-national" soccer at representative level. The uneasy experiment extended to the clubs, including Cape Town's Hellenic. Teams would now be classified in terms of ethnicity, but could have three players from other "nations" (read as "races").

Change was in the air, the dynamic aided and abetted by an assortment of polished English international stars like George Eastham and a group of top German players who had been suspended in the Bundesliga following allegations of bribery. These outsiders soon made their mark as top dogs, and lifted footballing standards in the "white" arena.

But black players and teams were maturing all the time. In 1974 the instantly and hugely popular Kaizer Chiefs, a rebellious off-shoot of Orlando Pirates (it had split off three years earlier), were beaten, by Hellenic, only in the two-leg final of what was known as the Chevrolet Cup. Chiefs had nearly made it to the very top. But racial loyalties were fierce, and tensions ran high.

Englishman Jack Taylor refereed the second leg of this watershed game, played at the Rand Stadium. Just months earlier Taylor had taken charge of the World Cup encounter, in Munich, between Germany and Holland when, despite the award of a controversial penalty to the hosts, he had to deal with fewer problems and less aggression than on his South African trip.

A riot and field invasion caused a 30-minute halt to the match and almost resulted in its abandonment. Chiefs actually won the second leg – and thus confirmed that the "winds of change" were indeed sweeping through South African soccer. But they could not make up the

deficit from the first leg. Hence the anger of the partisan crowd.

However, the warning signs of disaster – of growing inter-racial hostility emanating from multi-national competition – were not immediately heeded and, following on the experimental Chevrolet Cup, the Football Association of South Africa – the then controlling body, dominated by whites – introduced a multi-national league at club level to replace the previously segregated competitions.

And soccer, for a while, degenerated into something as rowdy and lawless as the Wild West so familiar to us from Hollywood movies.

Meanwhile, the popularity of the once-dominant National Football league under the control of Vivian Grainger, Dave Marais and Syd Chaitowitz had begun to wane. Attendances were falling, and white clubs were struggling to meet their financial commitments.

WHITES PULL OUT

All this paved the way for the introduction of genuine multi-racial soccer in 1977.

But, once again, the changes were not made in a manner best suited to the needs and welfare of South African football as a whole.

Instead of a nationwide, equal and mutually valuable partnership between whites and blacks, the white-controlled FASA and NFL virtually abdicated, surrendering their authority to the black-dominated South African National Football Association (SANFA) and the National Professional Soccer League (NPSL)

The latter, though, benefitted enormously. The majority of top NFL clubs, among them Highlands Park, Lusitano, Hellenic, Wits University and Arcadia, joined teams like Kaizer Chiefs, Orlando Pirates and Moroka Swallows to create what was, instantly, a vibrant and rejuvenated NPSL.

Some of the NFL clubs, however, broke ranks and linked up with the traditionally non-racial South African Soccer League, only to realise there was no way they could compete with the numerically dominant NPSL. Within two seasons, Durban City and Cape Town City had joined their erstwhile colleagues in the NPSL. But unhappily only a small handful of

ABOVE *Whiz-kid Nelson "Teenage" Dladla in action for Chiefs against Highlands Park in one of the early non-racial games, in May 1979. The Amakhozi of that year rank as one of the best ever.*

ABOVE *Doubting Thomas – Scots-born Highlands Park coach Joe Frickleton initially believed white teams would always have the edge over their black opponents.*

ABOVE *Thomas Hlongwane, one of the stars of Moroka Swallows in the early 1980s. The "Beautiful Birds" were coached by Chilean-born Mario Tuani, under whose guidance the 1979 Chiefs team had scaled the heights.*

white administrators, men like Raymond Hack, Ronnie Schloss and Hellenic's George Hadjidakis, did not shirk their duty. These few, these too few, threw in their lot with what was effectively the changing of the soccer guard.

The first multi-racial NPSL soccer league, played in 1978, was, ironically, won by Lusitano, a Portuguese-controlled club with a fiercely partisan following. Lusitano were owned by local liquor tycoon John de Canha but coached by no-nonsense Scots-born Joe Frickleton – who would later confirm his reputation as a coach with the Midas touch by achiev-

ing notable successes with Kaizer Chiefs, Highlands Park (which he had played for), and Orlando Pirates. De Canha, together with former NFL chairman and property development mogul Michael Rapp and insurance innovator Monty Schapiro, featured prominently in the administration of the NPSL in the early days of the multi-racial League – alongside the autocratic George Thabe, Cyril Kobus, Gilbert Sekhabi and Rodgers Sishi.

SA SOCCER'S GREATEST

But in the late 1970s and early 1980s everything was focused on the spectacular rise of the non-racial club. The clubs had simply abandoned the old "multi-national" approach and recruited players, and played, without any regard to quotas. The move towards wholly mixed status – despite the gradual dilution of white influence off and on the field – proved to be a pioneering one in the elimination of apartheid, and, what's more, in demonstrating to the politicians how it should be done.

In 1979, under the guidance of the wily Chilean-born coach Mario Tuani, Kaizer Chiefs rose to new heights when they won the League and Cup "double" with what many regard as their greatest team. Indeed, with a squad that included the irreplaceable "Ace" Ntsoelengoe, "Computer" Lamola, Jan Lechaba and Abednego Ngcobo, as well as a gangling youngster by the name of Nelson "Teenage" Dladla (also fondly known as "Botsotso"), the Amakhosi of 1979 vintage must rank as one of the best sides that South Africa has ever produced.

Comparable, perhaps, was another scintillating side moulded by that self-same Tuani four years later, when the Chilean coach, acclaimed as "The Godfather", was at the helm of Moroka Swallows and "The Beautiful Birds" dazzled all and sundry with a squad made up of such luminaries as Thomas "Who's Fooling Who?" Hlongwane, Joel "Ace" Mnini, Aubrey "The Great" Makgopela, Sam "Happy Cow" Mnkomo, Johannes "Chippa" Molatedi and Aaron "Road Block" Makhathini.

Not to mention the seasoned defensive trio of Chilean professionals comprising Mario Varas,

ABOVE *Goalmouth action in a 1980 match between Swallows and Highlands Park.*

Raul Gonzalez and Eddie Campodonico. It would be a hazardous undertaking indeed to try and assess which has, in fact, been the greatest of all South African club teams, but the top five can probably be classified without too much trouble – the Highlands Park combination of the mid 1960s, Hellenic (with the help of a foreign invasion) in 1971, Chiefs in 1979, Swallows in 1984 and the Sundowns of the Ernest Chirwali, Harris Cheou, Sizwe Motaung and Chippa Masinga era.

And, with South Africa forging towards normality as apartheid finally began to crumble in the early 1990s, soccer made a fateful, problematic move from Ellis Park to the newly erected First National Bank (FNB) stadium in the Crown Mines area.

The hasty construction of the ground resulted in numerous shortcomings and it failed to ignite the same kind of atmosphere as Ellis Park – despite the fact that it was a great deal bigger and able to seat 80 000.

CHAPTER 5

DEATH OF AN ALL-WHITE LEAGUE

After operating in a domineering fashion for more than a decade, the race-based National Football League simply faded away, unnoticed and unloved. Its demise surprised no-one.

THE NATIONAL FOOTBALL LEAGUE, a body which, from 1959, ran a professional soccer league consisting of only white teams, came to an end in 1977. But not dramatically – after burning bright for the whole of the 1960s and part of the 1970s, it simply fizzled out, faded away from lack of attention. Its demise did not come suddenly, nor did it surprise anyone.

Why such a once-vibrant league ran out of steam remains a bit of a mystery – few statistics and facts about it have been recorded. But there are plenty of theories, the most convincing perhaps holding that the League simply failed to sustain the support of the white community it had attracted for so many years.

Former Highlands Park and Orlando Pirates coach Joe Frickleton was part of the NFL era. He joined Highlands as a player from Scotland's Glasgow Rangers in 1964 and has been involved in local soccer ever since as a coach – and an administrator with the now-defunct Bophuthatswana Professional Soccer League (Bopsol), of which he was general manager. Why did the NFL fold up like a worn pack of cards? Well, Frickleton says, the clubs, "in an attempt to recapture the lost fans who had been drifting away from the game, kept bringing out mediocre foreign players to boost the league. That failed dismally and the paying customers saw through that ruse. The fans wanted to see their local heroes, not pay good money to watch a bunch of very average foreigners taking over. The people simply stopped coming to our games".

I watched Highlands play in the old National Football League to packed houses, and even in the early days of the NPSL the all-white clubs could still attract bumper crowds. But sadly Highlands – like Durban City, Durban United, Cape Town City, Ramblers,

OPPOSITE *Chiefs' Shaka Nqcobo in a goalmouth tussle with Dave Waterson of Wits in 1985 Mainstay Cup final. The Students are one of the few originally all-white clubs to survive the years.*

Rangers, Maritzburg City, Port Elizabeth City, Berea Park, East London United, Maritzburg, Lusitano, Jewish Guild, Southern Suburbs, Olympia, Corinthians, Powerlines and Germiston Callies – declined with the collapse of the National Football League and have long since joined the dodo.

REMNANTS OF THE PAST

The only two survivors from the National Football League left in the current Premier Soccer League are Wits University and Hellenic. Callies were given what many believe was a raw deal: they were promised a place in the new NPSL but when the teams were drawn up for the first ever South African non-racial league, the promise was broken and the club's name left out. With no future left, owner Abe Ephron decided to cut his losses and close a club that had once enjoyed healthy support at its famous Driehoek ground.

Wits University played a key role in the transformation process. They saw the writing on the wall long before the demise of the National Football League. The club president, Professor Ronnie Schloss, was heavily involved with the running of the NFL and made no bones about the fact that change was inevitable. The Students were the first white team to advocate change and to play in the then black-controlled National Professional Soccer League.

Recalls Schloss: "We were way ahead of the politics and the government of the time. When one considers that it was back in the 1970s that Wits and the NFL decided to join the then black NPSL it shows that at the time the people running white soccer had at least a vision of the future. We realised that we needed to normalise soccer in this country or else future generations would never get the opportunity to play international soccer. It was the correct decision.

"We took a decision to leave the NFL whether it folded or not. Sure, crowds were going down but that was not our main reason

ABOVE *Time out . . . Dave Snaier headed the now defunct all-white National Football League.*

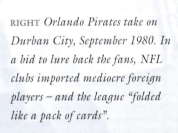

RIGHT *Orlando Pirates take on Durban City, September 1980. In a bid to lure back the fans, NFL clubs imported mediocre foreign players – and the league "folded like a pack of cards".*

for joining the NPSL. There was a split in the NFL and we believed rightly that the future of the game lay with the normalisation of the game. In other words every player should have the freedom to join which club, and type of players he wished to play with, without interference from the government.

Professor Schloss explains that in those days white football's controlling body, the Football Association of South Africa, (FASA), tried to stop clubs and players defecting to the NPSL by refusing permission for those clubs to play on FASA-controlled grounds. But, as Schloss points out, "We were fortunate in that as Wits University we owned our own grounds so we were able to form junior sections plus accommodate all the players at the university. We had over 2 000 members and the club became one of the biggest in Africa if not in the world, and we're still going strong."

He goes on to describe the NFL as a "very

tough and competitive league" and adds that "there were a lot of good players around in those days. I can remember derby matches against Highlands Park on the Republic Day holiday. The police told us to close the gates at 12:30 pm as the ground was full to capacity. It's hard to believe that white fans could fill any stadium in South Africa but it was a fact".

The Wits president remembers another occasion which was not so pleasant. "I think it was in 1976 or '77, just after the Soweto riots, we played Kaizer Chiefs in a friendly at Orlando stadium and the entire Wits team and management were arrested. In those days if whites wanted to play sport in the townships then one had to have a permit to do so. We did not get a permit and were subsequently arrested. With us that day was former Scottish international Pat Crerand who was guesting for us. I had my two young sons, then aged two and four, with me. The toddlers were also arrested. We were eventually released without charges being laid. That incident illustrates the problems facing both black and white clubs in their quest to normalise South African soccer."

The other incentive for Wits to join the NPSL was the possibility of benefiting from the enormous crowds the NPSL clubs attracted. Schloss ends on a saddish note: "Joining the NPSL did boost our gates and crowd support for a time, but today we see crowds again dwindling away."

NORMAN ELLIOTT REMEMBERS

One of the most colourful characters from the NFL era, and a founder member of the league, is Norman Elliott – who has no doubt that apartheid killed off both his club, Durban City, and the NFL. "Because of the government's racial policies we could not build up a following of black supporters," he says. "They simply were not allowed at the games, never mind getting them to play with or against us way back in 1959 when the NFL was formed or in the 1960s. I had to rely on white, coloured and Indian support."

Elliott adds that "We used to get raided regularly by the South African Police at our matches. I was able to squeeze only about 400 black fans into City's matches by claiming they were ground cleaners – this the SAP accepted but it

was far from a satisfactory situation." One of those so called "cleaners", recalls Elliott, was Lawrence Ngubane, who has been around the block in local football with AmaZulu, Bush Bucks and Orlando Pirates and now Manning Rangers.

But the man who brought the NFL to life and who sustained it was its general manager, the late Viv Grainger, who was also a respected sports journalist. Grainger worked tirelessly to get the fledgling league off the ground. He was in charge of the fixtures, he ran the league, he was its driving force. "Viv nagged and nagged

ABOVE *Viv Grainger (right), sports journalist and NFL general manager, worked hard and, as it turned out, fruitlessly to sustain the league. Here he greets Kaizer Motaung.*

ABOVE *The visionary Norman Elliott. His Durban City joined the SASF but later switched to the NPSL, which drew bigger crowds.*

LEFT *Police bombard fans with teargas outside the Rand stadium in 1978. The occasion: a needle match between Kaizer Chiefs and Lusitano.*

ABOVE *Kaizer Chiefs Elkim Khumalo (left) is challenged by Jerry Sadike of Pimville United in a 1973 game.*

me to join. He bombarded me with five phone calls a day and eventually I flew to Johannesburg and became one of the NFL's founding members," recalls the 75-year-old Elliott, who retired from running a soccer club after Durban City closed its doors in the 1980s.

Elliott has the distinction not only of helping found the NFL but also of founding two famous though now defunct teams – Durban City and Durban United. "I formed both City and United and entered them in the league," he recalls, "but was told that no person could own two clubs. I reckoned that was fair enough and had a plan to off-load United and gain a new ground for the NFL." Way back in 1959 the FASA, a white-run organisation that was unhappy that a professional and non-racial league was being formed under their noses, forbade amateur clubs to allow professional (NFL) clubs to play on their grounds. But Elliott did not earn the nickname "The Silver Fox" for nothing.

"That got me thinking about killing two birds with one stone," he remembers. "I went to Reg Johnson, who was chairman of the South African Railways Recreation Club, and he was a big help. I then managed to convince Hoy Park to become owners of Durban United and they agreed, which meant that NFL clubs could use Hoy Park, which was not under the FASA or Natal Football Association's control. I did the right thing in forming City and United as my plan was to prevent all the top Natal players from leaving the province and going to Johannesburg to seek their fame and fortune. Instead I was able to offer the players a home with either City or United. We never looked back during those years in the NFL. We had a lot of good times and as I see it the PSL could learn from those days."

Elliott looks on with a certain amount of envy at all the money being pumped into professional soccer these days. "We had very little money from sponsors and there was of course no television back then. I simply cannot believe the backing the PSL gets from TV and sponsors, it's tremendous.

"Sometimes I used to go cap in hand to the bank to get an advance for the players' wages.

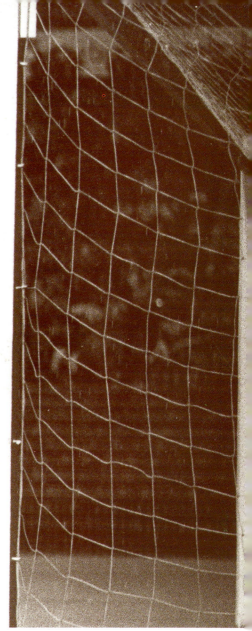

ABOVE *The acrobatic "coloured" goalkeeper Vincent Julius was recruited by top NFL club Arcadia to bring back the crowds.*

The reason I was successful was because I could tell the bank that within a week we would be playing either Highlands Park, Hellenic or Durban United and the money would be covered from the gate takings." And the talent was there, perhaps as good as any on show today. For example, the greatest of all South African goalkeepers, Elliott thinks, was City and Highlands Park's Tony Macedo. "Tony came out from England and proved to be a simply brilliant 'keeper," he says. "I rate him alongside the very best I've ever seen."

Syd Chaitowitz was the treasurer of the NFL. The first chairman was Dave Marais. Both men played a leading role in the development of professional soccer in this country (albeit in the white community), though it is sports journalist Vivian Grainger who is remembered, by most knowledgeable football lovers, as being the NFL's leading light.

But, as we've seen, the writing was on the wall as early as 1970 – support for the all-white league was dwindling. In an effort to combat falling attendance, clubs started fielding black players. Arcardia, one of the great sides in the NFL days, brought in Vincent Julius from the nearby Pretoria coloured township of Eersterus. Highlands recruited Jerry Sadike and Kenneth "The Horse" Mokhojoa.

It was a sad case of far too little, far too late, and the spectators, for the most part, stayed away – a far cry from the NFL's heyday, when 30 000-plus fans would swamp King's Park to watch Highlands and Durban City battle it out. "Yes, those were the days, and the soccer was top notch," Elliott reminisces.

CHAPTER 6

AFRICAN SOCCER: THE GOLDEN YEARS

The Seventies was a time of great names and great skills, of players who could change the whole course of a game with a single deft pass, and who became national heroes.

THE 1970s WAS THE GOLDEN ERA of black football; a period graced by skilful, inventive and committed players and by supercharged competition.

Backed by fairly good administrators, the quality of African soccer drew attention away from and thus contributed to the end of the white National Football League (see also Chapter 5).

More and more fans came to support the vibrant National Professional Soccer League.

This period witnessed the beginning of the end of the careers of Kaizer Motaung and Percy "Chippa" Moloi, and ushered in emerging stars such as Patrick "Ace" Ntsoelengoe of Kaizer Chiefs, Orlando Pirates' Ephraim Jomo Sono, Pretoria Callies' Mecro "Masterpieces" Moripe, Cedric "Sugar Ray" Xulu of Zulu Royals, Joel "Ace" Mnini of Moroka Swallows and Chris "Roll-away" Ndlovu of Pimville United Brothers. These players could change the fortunes of a game with only one deft move or pass. They became national heroes.

It was a time when the likes of Chiefs' manager Ewert "The Lip" Nene could sell ice to Eskimos with his smooth talking, and Elijah "Boy Baarde" Nhlapo and his Swallows cohorts would stop a game mid-stream, forcing the ref to abandon it, when their team was on the receiving end.

And it was also the time when the well-organised National Professional Soccer League (NPSL), under the chairmanship of South African Bantu Football Association (SABFA) president George Thabe, came of age.

OPPOSITE *The "Black Prince" – Matsilelete Ephraim Jomo Sono, one of the greats to emerge in the Golden Seventies, outwits an opponent with his sublime skill. Sono belonged to a handful of stars elevated to the status of national hero.*

NEW CLUBS, CUPS AND LEAGUES

A forerunner of the National Soccer League and the Professional Soccer League, the NPSL was established a year after Thabe defeated Bethuel Morolo as SABFA president.

Morolo had envisaged an "airborne league" in 1970. For the first time in black football history, clubs would, where the distances warranted, be flown to their fixtures.

But suspicions that Morolo was backed by the white Football Association of South Africa and the NFL in a bid to stall the former's impending expulsion from Fifa moved the politically conscious to ground the airborne idea.

The NPSL was founded through the efforts of a number of bodies and individuals, among them Pretoria's Bantu Callies and Mamelodi X1, Bloemfontein's Celtic and Mangaung United, Kimberly's Dalton Brothers, Natal's Lamontville Golden Arrows and Zulu Royals, Gauteng's Moroka Swallows Big XV, Pirates, Chiefs, Real Katlehong, City of Germiston, Vaal Professionals of Vereeniging and Witbank's Black Aces.

With George Thabe at the helm, the league received financial help from South African Breweries – which bankrolled the league championship called Keg – and from United Tobacco Company, which chipped in by sponsoring the Life Cup, named after one of their cigarette brands. In the following year, 1971, BP Southern Africa financed a knockout cup, called the BP Top 8, contested by the top eight teams on the previous season's final league table.

Chiefs – founded in 1969 by Kaizer Motaung, not as a formal club but as a select group of players expelled from, and supporters who grudgingly abandoned, Pirates in the previous year – were nearly excluded from the NPSL. Morolo had decreed that no selected team could take part in the envisaged "airborne league". The matter was resolved when "Kaizer's X1" was renamed Kaizer Chiefs.

ABOVE *The pathfinders. Pictured are Kaizer Motaung (squatting, third from right) and his Kaizer's XI select side, which set the ball rolling for the launch of Kaizer Chiefs. Others in the group include manager Ewart Nene (standing, second from right), and Ariel Kgongoane (standing, far left), who played for the all-black South African XI.*

On the recommendation of Matthew Mphahane, president of the Nigel Football Association and a close confidante of George Thabe, Chiefs affiliated to the NFA, who recommended them to the NPSL.

Pirates won the inaugural competition and repeated their triumph in 1973. Royals won it in 1972, and Chiefs in 1974. In fact 1973 was a vintage year for Pirates, who swept the board by winning the League, the Life Cup, the Top 8 and the Champion of Champions.

Chiefs, for their part, had won the transitional Stylo Cup in 1970 and, with players such as Ntsoelengoe, Ariel Kgongoane and Joseph Setlhodi, they simply had to go places. In 1972 they captured the Life Cup and the Champion of Champions and were runners up to Pirates in the League and Top 8, and were also crowned the UTC Super Team of the year.

Competition was stiff. Most clubs had acrobatic goalkeepers such as Chiefs' Sethlodi Banda, PUBS' Benjamin Mfundisi, Arrows' Henry "Black Cat" Cele (later also to achieve stardom as television's Shaka Zulu) and Royals'

Frederick "Cat" Mfeka. Isaac Manyaka of Professionals, Welcome Jama and Mozambican Jimmy Bene of Swallows, Peter Sejake of Benoni United and Chiefs' reserve Obed Dlamini came a close second.

On the pitch Ntsoelengoe, Motaung, Sono, Xulu, Moripe, Dinini Mwandla of Arrows, Alfred Mgedeza of Real Hearts and later Pirates, held fans under a spell with their superb skills, their flair with the ball complemented off the field by the vibrancy of managers such as Nene, Bethuel Masondo of Royals, Jimmy Sojane of Pirates, Jack Sello of Swallows and Henry Mhlongo of Aces.

Matches between Chiefs and Pirates or Swallows drew the biggest crowds anywhere in the country – as they do today.

TRAGEDIES AND TRIUMPHS

The National Professional Soccer League grew in popularity, but there were setbacks. Allegations of mismanagement and corruption surfaced in some quarters. There was also an element of personal tragedy.

Pirates' chairman Aggrey Mbatani was killed when the minibus he was travelling in – he was returning from a friendly match in Parys – overturned. Banda and the defenders Ronnie Shongwe, Ephraim Mashaba and Solomon Padi were among the injured. Nene was knifed to death in Springs while scouting for Nelson "Teenage" Dladla, who was to play a pivotal role in Chiefs' fortunes in later years. Bucs' chairman Washington Mposula was shot dead in his home in 1976 while heading a commission of inquiry into irregularities in the NPSL. Bucs' James Mabaso and Jack Sello were also targeted.

Not all the deaths, though, were violence-related. Jimmy Sojane of Bucs and Sello died of natural causes years later. And Masondo left soccer to concentrate on his thriving taxi business. But where there is money there is bound to be skullduggery, real or imagined. For instance Banda claimed, in September 1972, that he was bribed by a rival club official with R120 and the promise of further payment if he allowed Pirates to lose. Pirates were leading by one when Banda let in a silly goal, enabling the rivals to equalise.

Ephraim "Shakes" Mashaba, a former Pirates and Swallows captain/coach and later mentor of the South African Under-23 – AmaGlug-Glug – remembers how important loyalty to home territory was at that time. Talented players from specific areas were expected to play for the local team or else . . .

In the 1970s Soweto's "Big Three", Chiefs, Pirates and Swallows, dominated the NPSL. In the NFL, Durban City, Durban United, Cape Town City and Highlands Park ruled the roost. Durban City, under Norman "Silver Fox" Elliot, won the Castle League title in 1970 and 1972, Hellenic were the victors in 1971, Cape Town City in 1973, Pretoria's Arcadia Shepherds in 1974 and Highlands Park in the following season. Cape Town City regained the Castle League title in 1976 and Highlands in 1977.

The same clubs also proved to be very tough for their opposition in the NFL. Cape Town City won the Castle Cup in 1970, 1971 and 1976, Durban City in 1972, Highlands in 1973, 1975 and 1977, Arcadia in 1974.

Mixed soccer finally became a reality in 1978 when some NFL clubs unconditionally joined the National Professional Soccer League (see page 32). The Portuguese-related club Lusitano became the first winner of the new competition.

BELOW *Avalon Athletic's Cedric "Sugar Ray" Zulu watches teammate David Thusi lose a head-to-head duel to "Danger" Moloi of Moroka Swallows.*

CHAPTER 7

THE REVOLT AGAINST GEORGE THABE

Blood flowed as South African football split apart, heralding the most violent period in the history of the local game. Central figure in the ongoing drama was George "Kid Action" Thabe.

THE FEBRUARY 1986 EDITION of *Sports Ace* magazine carried a double-page picture of Bobby Makwetla, then marketing manager of King Foods, resplendent in a cream African dashiki with distinctive embroidery on the collar and sleeves.

Also featured was the then Putco AmaZulu captain Gaga Madlala, who is embracing the club chairman, flamboyant Jabu Phakathi, while the former el supremo of South African football, George "Kid Action" Thabe, rigidly stands to attention in a grey pin-striped suit, snow white shirt and matching grey tie.

The magazine was covering events at the George Goch stadium; the occasion was the King Korn Cup final, and AmaZulu had just defeated The Birds 4-3 to win the trophy. A closer look at The Birds and AmaZulu teams, however, indicates that the sides, although fully attired in maroon and green respectively (traditional colours of two of the most famous names in South African football) were not the real thing. They were shadow teams, playing in the colours of the big-name clubs.

A TIME OF VIOLENCE

The Birds and AmaZulu were splinter groups that emerged following the bloody split that, in the summer of 1984, changed the face of South African football forever. Among other new names of this

ABOVE *Thabe resisted the demands of the "rebels", and fought fiercely to the end like a wounded old buffalo.*

OPPOSITE *A dramatic moment in a Cosmos vs Pirates match in the mid-1980s. At one point two Pirates teams took to the field at the same time.*

traumatic period nearly two decades ago were Orlando Pirates, Ace Mates, and Vaal Professionals.

Blood flowed freely and lives were lost as South African football, splitting apart, went through the most violent period in the history of the game. Father turned against son, brother against brother, and the real issues affecting soccer got clouded over in the confusion.

Among the grimmest incidents was that in which enterprising China "Dibaba" Hlongwane suffered multiple stab wounds in a premeditated attack by a group of knife-wielding men. They had descended on the former Orlando Pirates official when, following bitter infighting, he led out a fully attired second or "alternative" Pirates' team (that is, there were two such teams on the pitch at the same time) to face Jomo Cosmos at Ellis Park stadium in the opening fixture of the 1986 Castle League championship.

The attack took place in full view of thousands of spectators and television viewers. Hlongwane fought back like an angry, frustrated bull in a Spanish festival, unable to gore a single one of the "matadors" who stabbed at him and then darted out of harm's way.

South African football entered a new era following the split and the subsequent birth of the South African Soccer Association, forerunner of the present South African Football Association (Safa). Eventually calm was restored; and some of the teams that made their appearance during that hectic period curled up and died; others survived as the situation returned to normal. Yet there was no doubt that the period left ugly scars that took a long time to heal.

And soon after the picture was published in *Sports Ace* (the magazine, like some of the teams of the time, has also since gone the way

ABOVE *Orlando Pirates and Jomo Cosmos fight it out in 1984, a year in which the winds of change were blowing hard.*

of the dinosaur) Thabe stepped down from his position as president of SANFA and as chairman of the NPSL. The decision was hailed as a step in the right direction, but observers shook their heads in sadness. The decision, they said, had come one year too late. Irreparable damage had been done to local football.

SOCCER'S WINDS OF CHANGE

Long before the split there had been growing concern among club officials who wanted to implement changes to the running of football in the country. They were especially concerned with marketing the game, and generating more income. But Thabe, who at that time held two influential positions – as chairman of the professional NPSL and president of the controlling SANFA – probably felt threatened and opposed the proposals they put forward.

But by 1984, the winds of change were blowing hard and clubs were determined to realise their ambitions. They called for Thabe to vacate his position as chairman of the NPSL (though they also urged him to retain his SANFA presidency). They secretly and perhaps grudgingly felt the Sebokeng schoolmaster

wielded too much power, and that they were losing out financially.

Today the club with a home fixture enjoys the luxury of collecting the *entire* gate returns, something that was quite alien during the reign of the one-time el supremo Thabe, who had put in place a system in which all gate takings were collected and taken to the NPSL offices for auditing. And, as chairman, he ensured that a certain percentage was levied on the takings, a further five percent deducted for ground tax, one percent for a Development Trust Fund and the rest shared equally among the clubs. Obviously this was not an acceptable arrangement to the majority.

But Thabe brushed off their demands.

The clubs also made it clear that they were not happy about the fact that Thabe drew salaries from both SANFA and the NPSL – which made him the highest paid official at the time – while they battled to keep the wolf from the door. The system was indeed flawed: even highly supported clubs like Kaizer Chiefs, who drew crowds of more than 40 000 to their games, took home figures in the region of R12 000 a week, sometimes even less!

Frustration set in as it became clear that Thabe was not prepared to relinquish his post as chairman of the NPSL, nor even listen to the grievances. Eventually Kaizer Motaung organised a group of rebellious club officials who drew up a petition calling for Thabe to resign. Motaung was ably assisted by Abdul Bhamjee, PRO of the league. Several sports journalists abandoned their tasks in their respective newsrooms and went on a crusade, recruiting clubs and persuading lower division club owners to attach their signatures to the petition.

The number of votes grew, and the petition was handed to Thabe who, in terms of the NPSL constitution, was now supposed to convene a special meeting to enable the clubs to decide, collectively, on a course of action. However, a day before the meeting Thabe, instead, called a media conference and announced he had no intention of entertaining the demands of "rebels". In any case, he added, they were supposed to give him notice "in terms of the constitution if they desired to call a special meeting".

The move succeeded – for a time. Thabe earned a temporary respite on a technicality, and the clubs retreated to the Kaizer Chiefs' offices, bruised and battered by a wounded old buffalo with its back against a tree and fighting a determined rearguard action.

CUT AND THRUST

Battle lines were even more clearly drawn when Thabe slapped Bhamjee with a banning order the following day, and then, going even further, summoned his deputy, Leepile Taunyane, and Motaung to a disciplinary committee hearing. The charges: bringing the league and SANFA into disrepute.

Nobody had in the past stood up to Thabe and got away with it. But Bhamjee, conducting himself as if "Kid Action" had not gagged him, simply ignored his banning orders and called a press conference. Motaung, for his part, rejected the order to appear at the disciplinary hearing, and then challenged Thabe to resign – a defining moment for South African football. The stage was set for a war to the bitter end.

SANFA's executive committee met behind closed doors to discuss the demand by clubs for autonomy and for Thabe to relinquish his post as chairman of the NPSL. They had proposed amendments to the constitution transferring power from SANFA to the NPSL. They also promised to donate a certain percentage of revenue to SANFA to run amateur football. Thabe proposed amendments to the constitution giving SANFA total control over football in South Africa. The two sides were deadlocked. The clubs gave Thabe a deadline of January 23 to resign or they would secede from SANFA. An unrepentant Thabe dug his heels in, claiming the constitution stipulated that SANFA appointed him chairman and, therefore, that only the organisation could tell him to resign.

Said Motaung at the time: "Thabe cannot tell us what to do and not do. It is the clubs that must decide their own destiny." Thabe refused to call the emergency meeting to discuss amendments to the constitution, claiming he had been given too little time.

On February 1, just a month before the new league championship was to get underway, the 18 clubs withdrew their affiliation to the NPSL. They went on to form the National Soccer League (NSL) and, later, also a new amateur body named the South Africa Soccer Association (SASA), with Solomon "Stix" Morewa at the helm.

Thabe called their bluff and optimistically vowed that, even in the face of such adversity, the NPSL would never die, that it would carry on, with or without the 18 teams.

Thus the NPSL splintered, giving birth to AmaZulu, Pirates, Kaizer Chiefs (formerly Ace Mates), Moroka Swallows (The Birds) and others. The NPSL continued to exist, though as a mere shell of its former self – you can fool some people some of the time, but after a while they realise where the real big-name stars are and shift their allegiance. The crowds steadily deserted the NPSL, which staggered on until 1990, when it was assimilated into the scheme of things. By then Thabe, the man many people blamed for the split that ushered in the present order, had long retired from active soccer.

ABOVE *Bobby Makwetla, marketing manager of King Foods, which sponsored the King Korn Cup under the auspices of the beleaguered NPSL.*

CHAPTER 8

SA SOCCER COMES IN FROM THE COLD

A special Fifa meeting, held in Zurich in July 1992, welcomed South Africa back as a member. After 30 years in the wilderness, the country had finally returned to the international fold.

IN OCTOBER 1988 the South African Soccer Association (SASA) and its professional wing, the National Soccer League (NSL), having set the ball rolling for soccer unity in the country, sent representatives to meet with the banned ANC at its Lusaka, Zambia, headquarters.

The delegation consisted of Solomon "Stix" Morewa, the late Rodgers Sishi and Kaizer Motaung. In Lusaka they met Thabo Mbeki and Steve Tshwete, future state president and minister of sport respectively..

The P.W. Botha government was astounded by soccer's bold move, but it stopped short of taking action against the three men. However, F.W. de Klerk, then minister of national education and sport, promised to "seriously consider meeting" officials for their apparent indiscretions. He never did. This was not surprising as rugby, for long the sport of the Afrikaner, had also been to Lusaka, and nothing had happened to *its* representatives.

TOWARDS UNITY

The soccer bosses were indeed heavily censured – but by the ANC, for their indiscretion in allowing top players from England to visit the country as part of a rebel tour in 1982. The exiled liberation movement made it clear to them that unless there was complete sporting unity and a majority government in the country it would be futile to seek international recognition, let alone affiliation to the various international bodies. It emphasised that sporting isolation was a key element in the struggle against apartheid.

The ANC also informed the three soccer leaders that African states – Zimbabwe, Zambia and so forth – resented the fact that some of their players were flocking south to the National Soccer League. Their clubs were not being either adequately consulted or adequately compensated.

A month after returning, SASA made contact with other soccer organisations, among them the South African National Football Association (SANFA), the South African Soccer Federation (SASF) and the Football Association of South Africa (FASA). SASA invited Tony Wilcox's FASA to affiliate its teams to the then popular Chappies Little League for players under twelve.

But the moves towards unity were frustrated, in particular by the Rama Reddy-led SASF, prompting Morewa to comment that "The SASF have always proved a stumbling block … I can honestly not see them agreeing to the formation of a single controlling body soon". Reddy insisted that his organisation was committed to unity, but the talks would have to be on a "principled non-racial" basis. SANFA's Goba Ndhlovu, on the other hand, had reservations of a different sort: SASA, he said, were "imposing" themselves on the other organisations.

Two years of talks by the four organisations had, it seemed, produced little except petty bickering. But then the National Sports Congress (NSC), led by Krish Naidoo, came into the picture. In November 1991, with NSC vice-president Mluleki George in charge, it engineered partial soccer unity. SANFA decided to stay out, claiming that it had been insulted by some of the SASA delegates.

APPROACHES TO AFRICA

In November 1990 the Association for National Olympic Committees of Africa (ANOCA) invited all sporting bodies to a meeting in Harare, Zimbabwe. The head of that all-Africa body, Jean-Claude Ganga, told SANFA that if they were refusing to join forces with Safa, "the train would leave them at the station".

Undeterred by Ganga's threats, SANFA continued posturing, confident that there could be no complete unity without them –

ABOVE *Lucas Radebe, future South Africa (and Leeds United) captain, battles Cameroon's celebrated Roger Milla in Bafana's first, historic international match. The year was 1992; South Africa won 1-0.*

which did not stop Safa from taking the first steps towards seeking recognition with the Confederation of African Football (CAF) in 1991. SANFA immediately issued a stern warning that such an approach without them would be futile. Safa responded that "we have begged and pleaded with SANFA to get onto the train. We have now decided to make an application for observer status to CAF, which is the first step towards full membership. CAF and Fifa are being kept up to date about the proceedings and they both agree that the path we have taken is the right one".

In July 1991 a CAF fact-finding delegation, led by president Issa Hayatou, general secretary Mustafa Fahmy and executive member Ismail Bhamjee, arrived in the country, raising hopes of a return to international soccer even though the conditions set by Fifa – of full one-person-one-vote democracy – were still in the realm of political negotiation.

Apart from urging full unity, Hayatou stated that his delegation was so impressed with facilities south of the Limpopo that it was possible – a remarkable prophesy, this – that South Africa could host the African Nations Cup in 1996 and the World Cup in 2006.

Hayatou urged the new body to submit their letter of application by September 1991 for consideration by the CAF executive committee and

ABOVE *Anthony Wilcox helped cement unity, allowing junior FASA teams to play in the Safa-run Chappies Little League.*

BELOW *Goba Ndhlovu (left), president of SANFA, and Reggie Feldman (right) of SACOS, meet with Sam Ramsamy (centre) to discuss SANFA's reluctance to enter unity talks.*

then, in January 1992, ratification by the CAF congress. He then emphasised that, although it was Fifa's prerogative to restore membership, the way back to international football would inevitably be through Africa.

CAF had set an August 1991 deadline for full unity but, with this fast approaching, SANFA again put the spanner in the works when they announced that their former president, George Thabe, would be part of the delegation. This raised the ire of some Safa members, who viewed the move as an attempt to stall the negotiations. But in mid-August Safa and SANFA announced that all obstacles hindering unity had been removed, and that the way was finally clear for the application to CAF to go through.

FINDING COMMON GROUND

The CAF meeting produced both a comedy of errors and a serious setback. Some of the Safa officials failed to get visas for the trip, others missed their flight to Cairo – and then, to cap it all, news came through that the application for membership of the African body had been turned down!

It emerged that CAF was unhappy because, according to documents they had received from SANFA, unity had not been achieved.

This came, of course, as a huge shock to Safa,

who accused SANFA of stabbing the organisation in the back. The soccer fraternity was further stunned when SANFA president Goba Ndhlovu confirmed his body's about-face, claiming that there had never been unity and they were not closer to unity now than they had been two months previously.

But then the two bodies found comon ground and things quickly turned around. On December 8, 1991, at FNB Stadium, both Safa and SANFA issued a statement confirming that soccer was finally united, and steps were immediately taken to re-apply to CAF.

In January 1992 a delegation chosen by Safa took a letter of application to the CAF congress in Dakar, Senegal. On January 10, a faint voice crackled on the telephone. It was the voice of Morewa. His welcome words: "We are back in the African fold." The general assembly of CAF had unanimously approved South Africa's membership, subject to ratification by the full Fifa congress. It was very much the return of the prodigal son: South Africa had been a founder member of CAF in June 1956.

At the Dakar meeting it was argued that, because apartheid South Africa had been expelled by a Fifa congress (in 1976) following the suspension imposed in 1966, it was also a Fifa congress which should formally accept the country back. This posed a serious dilemma, and, apparently, a setback too, as the next Fifa congress was only scheduled to be held just prior to the 1994 World Cup finals in the United States. But a special Fifa meeting, held in Zurich in July 1992, made a special concession and provisionally accepted South Africa subject to ratification by the full congress in 1994. In the meantime, the country was allowed to participate in CAF and Fifa events. At last, after 30 years in the wilderness, South Africa was back in the international fold.

WINNERS AND LOSERS

Once the controlling bodies were fully merged the three professional groups – the National Soccer League (NSL), affiliated to SASA; the Federation Professional League (FPL) to SASF, and the National Professional Soccer League

(NPSL) to SANFA – had to follow suit. The Football Association of South Africa (FASA) did not have a professional wing after its league, the NFL, collapsed in 1978 so top clubs like Wits University, Arcadia Shepherds, Highlands Park, Durban City, Hellenic, Cape Town City, Germiston Callies and Lusitano joined forces with the then NPSL.

It was agreed to retain the name National Soccer League for the new, unified body. The NSL was the dominant group, bringing all 18 of their clubs to the top table, while the FPL could only bring six – Bosmont Chelsea, Santos, PE Blackpool, Real Taj, Manning Rangers and Crusaders.

The rest of the clubs were integrated into the Second Division.

But the real losers were the NPSL, who initially demanded that ten of their clubs be considered for the First and Second divisions – a demand strongly rejected by the NSL clubs, who offered just four places. This figure was later reduced to two places, and eventually not a single one of the NPSL teams were accepted into the NSL's top flight.

Mluleki George stepped down as interim chairman of the unified body; and in 1992 Professor Lesole Gadinabokao was elected first president. Gadinabokao's "cabinet" consisted of vice-presidents Molefi Oliphant, Ashwin Trikamjee, and Danny Jordaan. Stix Morewa was appointed general secretary.

BELOW *Santos's Duncan Crowie – here sent flying by Orlando Pirates' Bernard Lushozi in the early days of racially mixed soccer. Crowie sacrificed a bright career in the struggle against apartheid.*

CHAPTER 9

RANDS POUR INTO SOCCER

After a slow start, sponsorship has taken off in South Africa. The latest agreement will ensure that professional football receives a handsome R100-million a year in television money.

SOCCER SPONSORSHIP IN SOUTH AFRICA may be years behind some of the multi-billion-rand European leagues. But it is certainly, and by a long way, the market leader on the African continent.

Television has taken pole position as the biggest revenue provider, with the latest contract leaping from R7-million a year in the formative period of the Premier Soccer League to R12-million in the next contract to be signed. Since then the size of the funding has grown by quantum leaps. The new R500 million contract, signed in 2002, will ensure professional soccer in this country gets R100-million a year in television money.

The figure, though, is somewhat deceptive: it includes the cost of commercial air-time, which simply means sponsorship in kind rather than hard cash. There is also assistance in the administrative area and, says Irvin Khoza, Safa's vice-president and former head of the PSL's sponsorship committee, "it is on the basis of all those calculations that an overall figure is given". Effectively, the Premier Soccer League will now be worth a R110 million a year, and this has dramatically reduced the income gap between the professional soccer wing and Safa, the national governing body (their income runs at about R120-million a year).

SABC'S TAKE-OVER

These figures reflect huge progress since the 1980s, when the SABC almost removed soccer from its screens. The public broadcaster's attitude at the time seems to have been that it was actually

Justice Sithole slides the ball during Chiefs' 2-0 win over Ria Stars in the final of the BP Top 8 competition. South African soccer gets around R100 million a year from television.

doing the game, and especially the National Professional Soccer League, a favour by screening matches. A subsequent referendum gave the powers-that-be a rude awakening. Black viewers voted overwhelmingly for the chance to watch the beautiful game on their screens.

The latest sponsorship represents a complete take-over by the SABC, enabling them to pocket every cent from screening rights sold to any other broadcaster.

Auckland Park now has exclusive rights to the League, the BP Top 8, the Telkom Charity and Coca-Cola Cups. They also have the first right of refusal on all Confederation of African Football (CAF) matches as well as the naming rights on the NSL Cup (previously the Bob Save Super Bowl). "That is why we sold them the rights for such a large amount of money," says John Commitis, who was part of the PSL team that negotiated the deal.

THE FIRST FUNDS TRICKLE IN

When the whole concept of sponsorship started at the beginning of the 1970s, the total "commercial" funds allocated to professional football was in the region of R3 000 a season. Then, around 1975, the general manager of the whites-only National Football League, Vivian Grainger, pushed up the overall NPSL sponsorship to an annual R10 000 or thereabouts. This he did by canvassing such companies as South African Breweries and United Tobacco, who already sponsored tournaments like the Life and later the Benson and Hedges (cricket) cups. Since then the SAB has consistently sponsored soccer leagues.

Grainger, though, had not contrived bigger

sponsorships for entirely the right reasons. Pressure against racism in sport had been mounting both at home and internationally, and Grainger's aim was to improve the quality of the black NPSL largely in order to sidestep criticism of the racial divisions in the national game.

After the referendum of the early 1980s (in which, as mentioned, the vast majority of respondents wanted to see football on the small screen) and the introduction of such role-players as National Panasonic, television entered the game in a big way, to the point where it promised to change the whole nature of the soccer industry in South Africa.

But a lack of understanding of sponsorship issues in the then national soccer governing body, the SA National Football Association (SANFA), proved a stumbling block. Apart from anything else SANFA was successor to the SA Bantu Football Association, which was widely regarded, simply from its offensive name, as a highly restrictive organisation.

SPONSORSHIP BREAKTHROUGH

In the event, money matters did move on but at a snail's pace, and it was only in 1997, when the PSL was formed along the lines of the English Premiership, that real funds began flowing in. At that point, the national broadcaster pumped in R22-million in terms of its first three-year contract with the new PSL, revenue that ensured clubs would get monthly grants of R100 000 each. The next contract rocketed revenue to a healthy enough R36 million, and monthly grants to clubs rose more than 100 percent.

Moreover, the formation of the PSL enhanced soccer as a brand not only at the higher level. Individual sponsors also came to the party at club level, put their money where their mouths were, and demonstrated real commitment to the

TOP LEFT *Up for grabs – brightly dressed women show off the BP Top 8 trophy at the media launch in July 2001.*
LEFT *The production team and cameramen are all set to cover the game, played at the Royal Bofokeng stadium, Rustenburg.*

ABOVE *Sundowns players in joyful mood after defeating QwaQwa Stars 2-0 in the 1999 Rothmans Cup final, staged at the Royal Bafokeng stadium.*

LEFT *David Kannemeyer of Ajax (left) overpowers Pirates' Steve Lekoela in a contest for the ball in the 2000 Rothmans Cup final. The match ended in a 1-1 draw; Ajax won the replay 3-1.*

game – a commitment that especially benefited fashionable outfits like Orlando Pirates and Kaizer Chiefs. Alpha Cement, for example, set a bench-mark when they did a deal with Pirates (who at the time lacked a strong title sponsor) which promised the club R5-million a season for three seasons. This was way past Kaizer Chiefs' Premier Milling sponsorship, which, at R1-million a season, had previously topped the funding list.

At national level, television received a boost when the likes of Vodacom came to the table in 1997. At that time the national soccer governing organisation, Safa – an amateur body – teetered at the edge of a precipice. The mobile phone company pumped in around R12 million a year,

so restoring the necessary balance between amateur and professional football. Vodacom then turned its attention to individual clubs, extending substantial sponsorships to glamour outfits Kaizer Chiefs and Orlando Pirates, whom they bankrolled for a record R60 million each over three seasons – the biggest South African sponsorship ever.

BREWER'S BONANZA

Television, meanwhile, continued to subsidise the South African Breweries' league sponsorship. The Brewers managed to negotiate a sponsorship deal carrying prize money that is far lower than the travelling costs of the 18 professional teams for the 17 matches they each play in a season. In

BELOW *Kaizer Motaung and Chiefs fans celebrate victory in the 2001 Coca Cola Cup final, played at the FNB stadium, Johannesburg.*

the contract before this most-recently signed deal, for instance, prize money totalled R4,5-million a season – compared to travelling costs estimated at between R5 million and R6-million a season. Thus, effectively, teams had to use part of their monthly grants from television to cover their travelling costs while the Breweries reaped the full branding benefit of the sponsorship.

The new deal, however, puts the effective SAB sponsorship figure at R24-million a year, though this, once administration and other non-cash benefits are subtracted, goes down to just over R20 million a year.

Which is not as nearly as much as it sounds, considering that each of the 16 teams will be playing a total 30 games a season – a guarantee of massive mileage for SAB, which will enjoy exposure in 480 games for its money. Compare this to sponsorships like the Coca-Cola Cup, where R12-million is pumped in per season for a competition that lasts just four rounds, and the inequality becomes quite obvious.

However, the powers-that-be at the PSL seem content. They certainly haven't thought fit to explain how SAB manages such favourable terms, contract after contract, while other willing sponsors are waiting in the wings for an opportunity to get in on the act. In general, local soccer sponsorship still has a long way to go compared to their English counterparts and the British television industry.

In England, BSkyB (the TV channel) alone contributed 30 percent of the Football Association sponsorship, or an average of R107 million per Premiership club, during the past few seasons. And remarkably, the FA has managed to maintain a balance between excellent coverage and the fan's desire to watch soccer live, at the stadium.

That ensures that, for all the money that comes in in the form of sponsorship, those unfashionable teams, struggling without significant backers, can still rely on the old kind of soccer revenue – gate takings.

The British strictly regulate the number of their live matches. In fact, they would rather export their product – to countries like South Africa, where, remarkably, English soccer is shown more than in England itself. English regulations stipulate that no Premiership match may be televised live on a Saturday. On Sundays, only two live matches are screened.

LEFT *Jomo Cosmos boss and coach Jomo Sono and People's Bank's Jimmy Manyi kiss the trophy after their team's 2002 Coca-Cola triumph.*

The British example could serve as a guide to South African soccer in its need to structure deals in such a way that other corporate bodies are given both incentives and opportunities to participate – and to strike that balance between good television coverage and over-exposure.

However, South African soccer should still consider itself lucky: the figures remain upward-bound at a time when some other codes are experiencing sponsorship withdrawals. Athletics, considered the flagship of the Olympic Games, are the most recent victims after Absa failed to renew a R44-million sponsorship that commentators had hailed as a virtual take-over. Absa had more or less monopolised all the national athletics championships; they even sponsored individual athletes at the Atlanta Olympics in 1996. The Commonwealth Games also experienced financial troubles recently, and there were fears that Team South Africa might end up not going to Manchester at all – until the government's National Sports Commission intervened.

Athletics South Africa's chief executive puts the whole situation down to a lack of a common vision in the country, a "uniformed approach from the stakeholders, government, sport and business. Soccer might celebrate for now, but the situation might still catch up, unless we follow the example of countries like Australia.

"There is no doubt," he goes on: "that the Australians have a common vision. Right now [in 2002] they are bidding for the Soccer World Cup and there is no dissenting voice. The same went for the Olympics in 2000 and they are hosting the next Commonwealth Games. We need a sports convention where we would come together with a common vision."

ABOVE RIGHT *Sizwe Motaung in action for Kaizer Chiefs in the 1997 Rothmans Cup final, played in Johannesburg. Chiefs beat Sundowns 5-4 on a penalty shoot-out.*
RIGHT *Leon Dipenaar of the Courier & Freight group (XPS), standing at right, and Safa's Danny Jordaan (left) announce their new partnership. XPS have pumped R2 million into South Africa's bid to host World Cup 2010. Koos Radebe stands in the middle.*

CHAPTER 10

BAFANA'S LEARNING CURVE

South Africa's first year in the international arena proved rough and tough, with defeats aplenty and rapid changes among both coaching staff and players. The eventual appearance of Clive Barker, however, made all the difference.

BAFANA BAFANA'S first steps into global soccer got off to an impressive start in the early Nineties, in a three-game friendly series against Cameroon.

The South African Football Association (Safa) had drafted in coach Stanley "Screamer" Tshabalala to guide the fledgling national team (this was after it was discovered that the incumbent, Jeff Butler, had embellished his coaching credentials) and Bafana went on to beat the "Indomitable Lions" 1-0 in Durban in July 1992 through a blistering penalty kick by Doctor Khumalo. Joy in the result, however, proved short-lived – two days later the South Africans went 2–1 down to Cameroon in Cape Town, before recovering their confidence and pride by drawing 2–2 in the final match, through goals scored by cousins Phil and Bennett Masinga, at the FNB stadium in Johannesburg.

But it got tougher as time went on. With the preparation for the African Cup of Nations (ACN) and World Cup qualifiers (WCQ) gaining momentum, Tshabalala simply could not string together a winning combination. The squad, led by captain Steve Komphela, was new and most players were still wet behind the ears as far as international competition was concerned. They found it extremely difficult to stamp their authority over their more experienced counterparts. Zimbabwe hammered them 4–1 in their ACN qualifier debut at the Rufaro Stadium, Harare, on August 16, 1992. The South Africans were no match for the star–studded Zimbabweans, who ran rings around Bafana's weak defence, comprising

ABOVE *A clear sign of early weakness – the fulltime scoreboard after the Bafana-Zimbabwe African Cup of Nations qualifier, 1992.*

OPPOSITE *Two years later, the same teams meet in a friendly; Bafana win 1-0. Lucas Radebe is seen shadowing Zimbabwe's Peter Ndlovu.*

Khambule, Lucas Radebe, Steve Komphela and David Nyathi. The visitors' only goal came through Sam "Ewie" Khambule.

Bafana were then handed their first loss at home, going down 1–0 to Zambia in another ACN encounter through an opportunistic goal (scored by the Mwape Mwiti, who later perished in that infamous crash along with his teammates near the Gabon coast) at the FNB stadium. The Zambians had outclassed Bafana; a dejected former Safa president, Solomon "Stix" Morewa, shed public tears after the defeat.

The dust of the Zimbabwean debacle had hardly settled when Tshabalala's squad were given another soccer lesson – an emphatic 4-0 drubbing by Nigeria in an away WCQ match in Lagos in October of the same year. So embarrassing was the score that the South Africans were branded as the "whipping boys" of African soccer by the rest of the continent.

ABOVE, LEFT TO RIGHT *The early bosses – Stanley "Screamer" Tshabalala, Bafana's first official coach; Jeff Butler, initially appointed national coach but fired for embellishing his CV; Peruvian-born Augusto Palacios, who took over in 1993, with dismal results. He was succeeded by the wily Clive Barker.*

BELOW *Mark Williams displays his African Cup of Nations winners' medal.*

As newcomers on the global football scene, Bafana inspired precious little confidence among their fans. Or respect from the rest of the soccer world. Under Tshabalala's less than illustrious tenure they had won just a single match – the very first one they played, against Cameroon.

CHANGES AT THE TOP

The shambles at the highest level of South African football led to the appointment of a German, Horst Kriete, as technical adviser to Tshabalala; and then, just when his hands-on skills were needed most, to Kreite's removal (a strange decision, this) and appointment as director of coaching; and finally to the the unceremonious suspension of Tshablalala himself – just three days before the WCQ match against Congo at the FNB stadium.

The last move seemed to work: Shakes Mashaba, Tshabalala's assistant, was roped in, temporarily, to steer Bafana to their Congo match. Bafana emerged 1-0 victors (through a Masinga goal). But by this time the squad was in a state of anarchy, some players showing total disrespect for the reinstated Tshabalala. This became evident when leading NSL goal-scorer Mark Williams said he would not play for his country unless Tshabalala was relieved of his duties. Captain Neil Tovey made an impassioned plea for Safa to adopt a more professional approach in its handling of the national squad.

THE PALACIOS ERA

Soon after the Congo match the Peruvian-born coach Augusto Palacios was drafted into the squad to steer Bafana into less troublesome waters – with little success.

The team's dismal performance continued when it played to a goalless draw against minnows Mauritius in the ACN qualifier at Rand Stadium on April 10, 1993, producing a shocking display of target shooting. Nor did their return ACN clash against Zimbabwe in Johannesburg two weeks later bring Bafana much comfort as they struggled before settling for a 1-1 draw – after a perfect shot from the boot of Marks "Go Man Go" Maponyane.

Palacios underwent a barrage of criticism from both the media and the soccer fraternity for his dubious selection policy as the build-up to the ACN second round match with Zambia reached

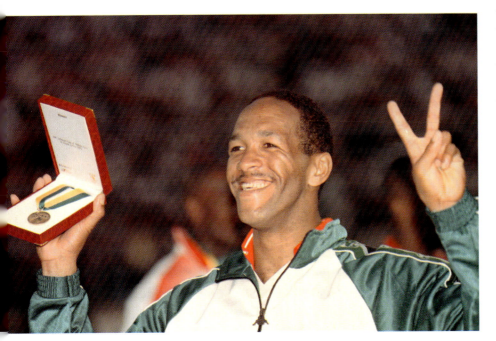

ABOVE *Bafana captain Neil Tovey leads his side out to confront Cameroon – the first in an historic three-match drawn series in July 1992.*

fever pitch. Spirits in the Bafana camp remained low, and it came as no surprise when they suffered an ignominious 3-0 mauling at the hands of the Chipolopolo at Lusaka's Independence stadium in July of the same year. The match marked goalkeeper Roger de Sa's international debut; the Zambians, playing brilliantly, made scoring goals look easy.

And so it went on, with an out-of-sorts squad clearly lacking direction and Palacios trying desperately for a winning combination. But the stage was too big for him.

Although Bafana posted a 3-1 victory over Mauritius in their last ACN qualification match, the coach's limitations were painfully exposed when Bafana were clobbered 4-0 by Mexico in a friendly game played, in Los Angeles, in October 1993. The horrendous defeat came despite the fact that the South Africans had prepared well for the match, and that they had in their ensemble players who were plying their trade overseas. Among the latter were Turkey-based John "Shoes" Moshoeu, Tebogo Moloi, Steve Komphela and Pitso Mosimane.

Palacios was summarily dismissed by Safa, and the suave and likable Clive "The Dog" Barker was brought in to guide the national team, hopefully to glory.

THE ROAD TO RECOVERY

The South African squad opened their 1994 soccer calendar by beating Zimbabwe 1-0 at home in an African Cup of Nations encounter (goal by Masinga) – a turning point, it seemed, and harbinger of things to come, for they then managed another triumph (2-1) over Zambia in

the Nelson Mandela inaugural match at Ellis Park stadium in May.

This was a very special occasion, the Independence game – national elections had swept South Africa's first democratically elected government into power, and the nation and its soccer stars were in the mood to celebrate. The match also marked the diminutive Barker's first appearance in charge, as the man entrusted with the daunting task of saving the national squad from total disgrace. His principal task was to transform Bafana – which had failed so dismally to qualify for the 1994 ACN – into a formidable force for the next continental showpiece. This was to be hosted by South Africa, in 1996, following the withdrawal of financially struggling Kenya as host country.

Although the squad began to click as a unit under Clive Barker, they went down in a two-match friendly series against Australia, played Down Under, in June 1994. Despite the loss

the players began to cultivate a sense of discipline and became more confident and more of an organised unit as time went on. The year 1995 saw more improvements as Barker introduced wholesale changes, bringing in a number of youngsters as well as recalling overseas-based players for Bafana's official games.

The days of being referred to as "whipping boys" and "no hopers" were soon to be just a nasty memory as the squad became more focused and found their winning ways. In the same year they registered an unbeaten run in six matches, winning three and drawing three.

What was remarkable is that the squad managed to draw against two top countries – Argentina (1-1) and Germany (0-0). All in all, Bafana Bafana went through hell during the formative stages of their international involvement, but managed a remarkable transformation prior to their historic African Cup of Nations victory in 1996 (see Chapter 14).

OPPOSITE *South Africa and Argentina battle it out in a 1995 friendly. The match was drawn (1-1) – an encouraging result for the ever-improving Bafana squad.*

LEFT *Jacob Tshisevhe and Australia's Damian Mori go head-to-head in September 1996. Remarkably, Bafana won the game (2-0).*

CHAPTER 11

SOCCER'S SHAME

The transformation of South African soccer has not been trouble-free. In particular, two major scandals – both involving people who helped liberate the country from its corrupt past – shocked the nation.

SOCCER'S GREAT MAKE-OVER has not been a smooth affair. Human weaknesses have played a significant and unwelcome role in the transformation process – notably in the context of two major scandals, in the early Nineties, that shocked the country to its foundations. An especially dismaying element was that they involved prominent individuals, indeed the very people who helped to liberate the country from the despotism and corruption of the past.

The scandals hit soccer where it hurt most, at the gates – fans felt deeply that they had been betrayed, so deeply that South African soccer is still to recover from the revelations. Add to this the accusations of money laundering (so far unproved but the rumours are rife all the same), and of nepotism and corruption, that bedevil the game. For instance, two officials were recently given golden handshakes when they left the league – after they had committed offences that warranted criminal investigation, or dismissal at the very least. All in all, the game has not covered itself in glory on issues of corporate governance and financial transparency. Government has also, apparently, been lax – it is still to take decisive action to root out corruption with and maladministration of the game. One of the reasons given for inaction concerns Fifa's regulations, which are very specific on the issue of government interference in the sport. Fifa intervenes as soon as government interferes in sport.

ABOVE *Former National Soccer League public relations boss Abdul Bhamjee – convicted on all but two of 33 counts of corruption, fraud and theft involving R4.7 million.*

OPPOSITE *While the scandals of the late 1980s and early 1990s unravelled, the Beautiful Game continued as usual – almost. Many disillusioned fans stayed away. Pictured is Kaizer Chiefs' Cleophus Dlodlo.*

THE MISSING MILLIONS

The first scandal resulted in the jailing of Abdul Bhamjee, public relations officer for the National Professional Soccer League, and Cyril Kobus, the PSL's chief executive officer, after a whopping R7,4-million was systematically siphoned out of the coffers of the League over a 40-month period dating back to 1987. Secondly, top administrator Solomon "Stix" Morewa was sidelined after a commission of inquiry ordered his removal because of serious discrepancies in the manner in which he ran Safa's affairs.

Bhamjee had entrenched himself as the PRO in charge of media liaison and marketing and worked closely with his CEO to develop the game. He went around clinching deals with sponsors and securing television rights with top South African Broadcasting Corporation executives. There had been persistent whispers that all wasn't above board. The first to raise concern was Leon Hacker, vice-chairman of the League. But Hacker received little support as many members of the NSL management committee rightly felt they needed documentary evidence to substantiate his allegations. Hacker investigated the alleged theft and forwarded his findings to the attorney general. The late former chairman of the NSL, Rodgers Sishi, was implicated, together with Cyril Kobus.

Bhamjee came before the Johannesburg High Court and was granted bail of a massive R100 000. He faced 35 counts of theft, fraud and corruption. Evidence before the court showed that he had managed to leach money out of the public affairs account, which he had single-handedly opened and managed, by altering the figures and pocketing the difference.

Next to face the music was Kobus, who was found guilty of embezzling R5, 2-million and sentenced to six years in jail. In the event, however, he served only 27 months.

RIGHT *Samuel Mdluli, alias Coloured Passmore, gave evidence in favour of Bhamjee, but his credibility was torn to shreds.*
FAR RIGHT *The NSL's Cyril Kobus (left), seen here with David Thidiela, the league's former chief of security, was sentenced to six years in prison for stealing R5,2 million.*

One of the issues that emerged in court was that Bhamjee showered journalists and prominent members of the public, those in influential positions, with gifts. In fact, a number of journalists were on his payroll. After being found guilty, he tried to bargain with the NSL, pleading in mitigation that he was offering to pay back R2-million. The League refused. Incidentally, in his judgment the judge lambasted the League for leaving Bhamjee solely in charge of the public affairs account with no checks and balances to safeguard their money. The judge further expressed disappointment at, and chastised the NSL for, the lack of financial control by allowing Bhamjee to run the public affairs department without any interference from its management committee. He also criticised the decision of the League to keep the sponsorship amount between the NSL and SABC a secret and pointed out that it opened the door for Bhamjee to commit theft.

The crimes were committed between 1987 and 1991, the whole sorry saga culminating with a conviction in February 1992. Bhamjee was sentenced to an effective 14 years in prison and a further six years imprisonment for stealing funds totaling about R660 000 from Premier Milling, a further six years for stealing R775 000 from the National Soccer League, and four years for the theft of R175 000 from Crusader Life Insurance Company (all these sentences are running concurrently).

League chairman Sishi, who died in 2001 aged 73, "earned" himself a mere R400 000 during that time, while chief executive officer Kobus scored a cool R5,2-million. Sishi, who turned state witness and testified against Bhamjee, admitted receiving his money in illegal payments from the public affairs accounts operated by the disgraced PRO.

MOREWA'S WRONG TURN

Sadly, Stix Morewa will be remembered only for his wrongdoing; few will recall the fine administrator, nor reflect on his commitment, hard work, dedication and the sacrifices he made for the benefit of the game.

Morewa's passion for football has never been questioned. Most notably, he was a key player in the establishment of a single, non-racial and united South African Football Association in 1991 following talks between rival organisations in the country (see Chapter 8) – one of the highlights of his career.

At 18 years of age and, together with the likes of Dikgang Moseneke, one of the youngest political prisoners on Robben Island, Morewa was detained without trial in terms of the notorious "90-day clause". He ended up serving three years on the Isle of Makana (as the inmates called the place), which is where he met president-in-waiting (now former president) Nelson Mandela. Mandela surprised Morewa in 1992, just after his release, when he recognised Stix in

FAR LEFT *Justice Benjamin Pickard – accused Morewa of selling soccer's assets for a song.*
LEFT *Solomon "Stix" Morewa – received a luxury German car in return for a sports marketing company.*
BELOW *Brian Mahon (centre), the charmer whose ASI enterprise allegedly grew financially strong from South African football. He is seen at a function, flanked by Alex Abercrombie and Kaizer Motaung.*

a delegation that included Raymond Hack, Kaizer Motaung and Abdul Bhamjee. The men had arrived to pay their respects to Rolihlahla at his Soweto home.

And it had been Morewa's tireless efforts that secured the 1996 African Cup of Nations tournament for South Africa – after designated host Kenya withdrew at the eleventh hour due to financial constraints. South Africa even won a prestigious award from Fifa as the best movers in the year 1996 – for their remarkable achievement in gate-crashing their way into the Fifa top twenty rankings, up from 78th position at the beginning of the year.

At the height of his career, perhaps flushed with the excitement of the new era and the success he had attained in the lead-up to and after 1996, Morewa self-destructed. He was busted by Judge Pickard for improper conduct. He was requested to resign his position.

Initially Morewa had described the Pickard Commission as a witch-hunt and a plot by certain individuals who, with the help of the media, were hell-bent on destroying him, but as the judge investigated and unravelled the affair it became apparent that Morewa had his hands too deep in the cookie jar.

The Pickard Commission found that Morewa had received a luxurious German car in return for favours to a sports marketing company that had usurped the powers and functions of Safa.

The judge also found that Morewa had deposited an amount of R500 000 into his personal account and, presumably in return, had naively signed away his powers to run the organisation and its events to the sports marketing company.

What makes Morewa's case even more tragic is the fact that the man was such a brilliant administrator, a charming and intelligent leader and a damn good orator to boot!

But as they often say, the show goes on. Whatever the scale of his contribution, the game is far bigger than any individual.

Perhaps, though, Morewa can retain a modicum of pride in himself, at least for planting the seeds of a garden that is now ready to be harvested.

CHAPTER 12

THE PSL IS BORN

A few years ago leading lights of local soccer remodelled South Africa's top professional competition on England's elitist and enormously successful Premier League. Is it working? It has certainly had its downside.

FROM A DISTANCE England's soccer scene looked like paradise. So in 1996, inspired by the boom brought about by soccer through the formation of the Premier League in that country, ambitious local officials like Kaizer Chiefs' Kaizer Motaung and Orlando Pirates' Irvin Khoza set about creating a similar, elite type of competition in South Africa, and in due course our Premier Soccer League, or in its abbreviated form the PSL, was formed and hoisted onto an unsuspecting public.

In essence, there was little change in formula from what had previously been known as the National Soccer League, or NSL. The teams were basically the same, the standard of football was the same, and the shortcomings had not changed much either. And local football was still dominated by massive, almost eerily overwhelming support for Chiefs and Pirates.

And this, in some ways, was the difference between the two Premier systems. The English one was balanced; the South African one was top-heavy. Chiefs could probably play Pirates every week of the year in any sort of fixture, and in any part of the country, and the crowds would fill the stadiums to capacity or near-capacity. Other sides struggled to attract spectators. Even the domination of Sundowns during the formative years of the PSL – the club won the Premier League title on three successive occasions – failed to make any dent in the popularity of Pirates and Chiefs.

Not so in England. Manchester United might be the most popular team in the world, but go to London and you'll find that the majority of soccer fans despise and deride the northern giants, and local sides are very well supported.

So there was no instant boom as there had been in England, no

OPPOSITE Chiefs' fans on a roll. The new league has been an improvement on the often confused past – but it has had its downside. It is unbalanced, dominated by just two massively supported clubs – Kaizer Chiefs and Orlando Pirates.

injection of mind-boggling riches, no astronomical transfer fees or dizzy increase in public support.

Nevertheless the business sector was quick to comprehend that the majority of South Africans still placed soccer second only to religion, and enough money was invested in the game by the likes of SABC and South African Breweries to make life reasonably comfortable for the Premier League clubs (see Chapter 9).

A far-reaching decision was also taken to start the official football season in August and run it through to May instead of playing over the entire calendar year. Once again this mimicked the English approach, and was supposed to benefit local soccer because the playing seasons in South Africa and Europe would now coincide. But weather conditions in the two hemispheres differ dramatically and to this day it is debatable whether this was a smart or counter-productive move.

But one thing is for certain: South African football is out-of-step with the rest of Africa, where a soccer season starts and finishes in the same year. This is a disadvantage to PSL champion clubs, which now have to wait an extended 18 months or so before participating in African competitions like the Champions League.

COMING AND GOING

Administratively, the changeover from the NSL to the PSL was designed to give greater power to the Premier League clubs through the formation of a high-powered board of governors in running affairs in conjunction with a dynamic, inventive and courageous Chief Executive Officer.

And herein lay problems for prime movers Motaung, Khoza, Hack and company. The board of governors has been largely ineffective because club officials, by and large, did not devote themselves from the start to working vigorously and sincerely for the game as a whole, preferring instead to make decisions based on sectional interests. Many members of the board, moreover,

appeared to have been too laid-back to make of the body a creditable, highly respected and dynamic forum.

As for the succession of CEOs, they have all had shortcomings of one sort or another. Most had no basic training or experience in either soccer management or the technicalities of the game.

Brought in to head things up was an English millionaire Trevor Phillips, who at one time held a prominent position in the English FA, and who projected an image of forthright even-handedness. He brought a degree of much-needed professionalism and know-how to the running of the PSL, while attempting to divorce himself from the special interests and power blocs that sought to dominate the organisation. And he produced some creditable results, such as the introduction of the Rothmans Cup. In time, however, his attempts to be his own man waned as he tried, unsuccessfully, to perform an ungainly balancing act in the hope of keeping everyone happy.

When Phillips left the PSL at the conclusion of his contract, in 1998, the organisation was generating an annual revenue of R60-million.

MORE CHANGES AT THE TOP

Joe Ndhlela was immersed in controversy long before his appointment as the PSL's chief executive officer. For this reason alone he should never have been employed as such. His initial backers became his fiercest detractors after his association with a rival faction within the League.

Enter Dr Robin Petersen, a sincere, well-meaning man (his doctorate was in Divinity) who had become involved in the realm of soccer administration only a couple of years earlier as part of Danny Jordaan's World Cup bid team. As CEO, Petersen seemed to have dreams of transforming the PSL into a soccer paradise - and came away second best after crossing swords with a demanding and not too helpful board of governors.

To compound Petersen's woes South Africa was confronted by its worst sporting tragedy on April 11, 2001 when 43 spectators died in a stampede during the Chiefs-Pirates derby match at Ellis Park. Petersen was hardly to blame for the disaster, nor for the organisational shortcomings that had built up over the years, but he was the hands-on boss, and everyone knew where the buck stopped.

The PSL, however, had not learnt its lesson and went on to appoint Petersen's successor Mandla Mchunu, a successful, livewire, innovative businessman but one with no real experience in soccer administration. Mchunu went on to fill a series of ill-defined positions at the helm of the PSL, mostly on what seems to be a spare-time basis, and in the process making the League and its board of governors look somewhat ineffectual.

Shortly afterwards the Premier League, at the instigation of Safa and vice-president Khoza, implemented a R16-million plan in terms of which the franchises of two clubs were bought and the number of teams reduced from 18 to 16. This was intended to ease the fixture congestion, but it didn't solve the PSL's basic malaise – too many competitions, too many friendlies, too many private events, too much greed all round.

It remains to be seen whether the latest CEO can tackle these basics and fine-tune the machine. The man in question is – Trevor Phillips, who returned to head the PSL at the end of 2002. In the interim years he had served as chairman of the Windsor racecourse in England.

Phillips set out the ground rules even before

taking up his appointment. "In my capacity I require authority," he told the media. "I must have all the conditions and tools required to succeed in this job . . . I would not have returned if my control was limited."

The PSL and Safa, he insisted, had to establish a working relationship, notably in regard to a sensible international fixture list – one that allowed the clubs to field their top teams on a regular basis. Players' rights, a subject that had led to confrontation with the PSL board of governors in the mid-1990s, also featured on his priority list. "Fans do not pay to see Phillips, Kaizer [Motaung], Irvin [Khoza] or Natasia [Tshiclas]," he explained. "They just want to enjoy the performances of their favourite players."

Soccer does have its problems. But then the game generally and the PSL in particular – despite all the shortcomings – is too popular, too revered, too big in South Africa to be seriously threatened. The show will go just on and on, irrespective.

ELLIS PARK – AND ITS LESSONS

We have touched on the enormous popularity of the Chiefs-Pirates confrontations, and on the disaster – perhaps inevitable disaster – at the huge Ellis Park stadium, and on the "organisational shortcomings that had built up over the years". What happened? Why did it happen? What can we learn from the tragedy?

On April 11, 2001, the two PSL sides squared up to each other shortly after 8.00 pm in a stadium that was full to overflowing. In fact, well before that time – at 7.15 pm – there were announcements that tickets were sold out. But nobody seemed to listen, and hopeful spectators continued to arrive, thousands forcing their way inside. Crowd control at the crucial perimeter fence (and elsewhere) appeared minimal; the rush for seats turned into a stampede, and the game was abandoned at 8.40 pm – by which time 43 people had been killed in the crush, more than 150 injured.

A year later Judge Bernard Ngoepe, in his interim report as head of the commission of inquiry, said that the "fundamental cause of the tragedy" was that nobody, but nobody, correctly estimated the pulling power of such a match and "No plans were in place to deal with a capacity crowd, let alone a crowd in excess thereof . . . All role players were remiss in not adequately taking previous experiences into account in their planning . . ."

There were other factors, too, plenty of them. Security was jeopardised because areas of responsibility hadn't been identified, and "there was no particular person in overall command" but instead a "collection of independent heads of security groupings, all of whom, to this day, deny that they carried the ultimate responsibility". There had also been downright "dereliction of duty" on the part of some officials, and a general failure to follow Fifa and Safa guidelines, especially the instruction that no game should start until there was complete control over the crowd situation both inside and outside a stadium. The public address system had proved inadequate; ticket sales were chaotic, and vehicle traffic around the stadium was congested.

All these factors contributed to the disaster. So, too, did the fans. "South African soccer spectators," said Judge Ngoepe, "need to appreciate that their own conduct is as critical a factor as any other in the maintenance of safety and security . . ."

ABOVE *Sports minister Ngconde Balfour and Pirates' chairman Khoza at Ellis Park just after the tragedy. The toll: 43 dead, 150 injured.*

BELOW *The game goes on as people die in the crush. Pictured are Kaizer Chiefs' Patrick Mbuthu (left) and Pirates' Dennis Lota.*

CHAPTER 13

SA FOOTBALL: THE FOREIGN FACTOR

The local game has been immeasurably enriched over the years by skillful ball-players from abroad. Most have come for honest and honourable reasons; a few for dubious ones.

THEY CAME (and still come) for all sorts of reasons – some arrived as rebel players, guests of local clubs, during the days of apartheid; others were in trouble with their overseas teams and their new hosts, the apartheid leagues, offered them shelter and the chance to pursue their careers; still others because they could earn more money here in South Africa than in their own, often very poor countries.

Of note is South Africa's fairly recent isolation from the world football controlling authority, Fifa, and from the continental body, the Confederation of African Football (CAF), a pariah status that enabled local clubs to sign on foreign players almost at will because the rules governing the movement of players worldwide were not applicable in South Africa. Also a factor has been the political instability in other parts of the continent, which has even led some foreign footballers to take out South African citizenship.

Current (2002) imports in South African soccer who immediately come to mind are Wilfred and William Mugeyi, the Zimbabwean twins who play for Bush Bucks in the Premier Soccer League, and their compatriot Gilbert Mushangazhike, who represents something of a nightmare for local goalkeepers. Kaizer Chiefs' sturdy defender, Patrick Mabedi, is a former Malawian international.

Meanwhile others, such as Nigerian striker Raphael Chukwu, Cameroon midfield marshal Roger Feutumba, Namibian cousins Mohamed Auseb and Robert Nauseb and a host of others have passed on to greener pastures in Europe. While many of them were worth something, some, like Cleopas Dhlodhlo of Zimbabwe and Ronnie Dube of Swaziland, were total flops.

OPPOSITE *Among the most talented of foreign imports has been Malawian midfielder Ernest Mtiwali (left), here playing for Supersport United. Some have been flops, most have added value.*

BIG NAMES IN SA

Some big European names were seen on our pitches during the apartheid era, among them former England star George Best, who came out as a guest of Highlands Park, and Eusebio, the 1966 Portuguese World Cup star. Eusebio was hosted in the 1970s by the once formidable side Lusitano. Other greats included English internationals Allan Ball, Derek Dugan, Bobby Charlton, Ron Davies and the late Budgie Byrne. Among those who decided to make South Africa their home are Walter da Silva, Joe Frickleton, Eddie Lewis, Mario Tuani, Jorge Santoro and Roy Matthews. They have made their names as coaches; some have coached most PSL sides; a few have become television commentators.

The trickle from Africa, which began in the early Seventies, flowed into the National Professional Soccer League and included the likes of Mozambique-born Jimmy Bene, who played for Moroka Swallows, and Kaizer Chiefs' Herman "Pele" Blaschke, who hailed from the then South West Africa (now Namibia). He was to be joined later by his cousin, Oscar Mengo, and his compatriot Pius "Garincha" Eigowab. Not to be outdone, Orlando Pirates took on Namibian Hendrik Hardley, who later moved to Manning Rangers. In due course fellow countryman Pius Eigowab, who had a stint with African Wanderers, joined him on the coast.

Kaizer Chiefs burnt their fingers when they brought in Brazilian World Cup soccer star Jairzinho. Chiefs were to part with R9 000 per game (a huge sum in those days) for all the four games in which Jairzinho was to appear, which meant he was earning about R90 per minute – if he played the whole 90 minutes in all four. But he failed to impress, and at the end of the visit Chiefs' management were left with a mini-revolt on their hands. The players questioned the wisdom of paying such a large sum of money to a foreigner while they were receiving "peanuts". They felt that, as people who

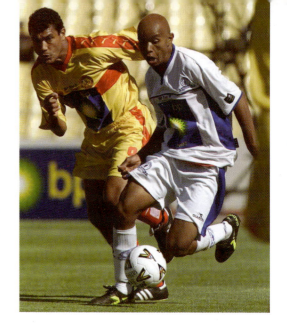

RIGHT *Sipho Nunens of Sundowns and Mauritian Marc Ithier (left) of Santos compete for the ball in the 2002 BP Top 8 final.*

had been loyal to the club for many years, any additional disposable income should have been shared among them.

Chiefs later employed the services of goal-getter Ebison "Sugar" Muguyo and sturdy defender Dan Chikanda, while Moroka Swallows signed up Oliver Kateya, George Shaya and Ernest Kamba. And in 1985 Bloemfontein Celtic won the Mainstay Cup fielding an almost all-foreign soccer team that beat African Wanderers 1-0 at a packed Ellis Park. Players such as Eden "The End" Katango, Ernest Chirwali and his cousin Cedric Nakhumuwa formed a combination that proved unstoppable.

The foreign-signing trend, which continued unabated, had both its advantages and disadvan-

tages. The outsiders, having been exposed to international soccer in their countries, brought in massive and much-needed experience, which was good for the domestic game. However, the downside was that the influx deprived local youngsters of places in the top teams.

CLUBS CAST THEIR NETS

The list is almost endless. Orlando Pirates brought to the country players such as Etienne Nsunda, Gento Kambala, both from the then Zaire (now known as the Democratic Republic of Congo), and at some stage the club also had Zambian striker Ackson Shimbala – known in his country as "Scud Missile" for obvious reasons – on their books. Later Pirates signings included Hendrik Hardley from Namibia (then known as South West Africa) and, most recently, Nigerian goalkeeper Okpara Williams and Guy Roger Nzeng from Gabon..

Other clubs soon joined in the rush. Players such as Zimbabwean Kennedy Nagoli, who turned out for Jomo Cosmos, have graced our shores. Cosmos also brought in colourful goalkeeper Mpangi Merikani – who entertained the crowds with his acrobatic stunts – from the Democratic Republic of Congo (DRC).

Among a number of good foreign players signed by Free State Stars have been the likes of Bunene Ngaduane and Emmeka Mamale, both also from the DRC; Burundian Nonda Shabane, the late Zambian striker Roger Lupiya, and a host of others.

Stars seem to specialise in foreign quality. Even Patrick Kazadi, though he ended up with

BELOW *Nigerian-born Raphael Chukwu celebrates his goal in the 1998 Rothmans Cup final.*

Orlando Pirates, was brought into this country by this enterprising club, as were the late Zorro Msiska, and the late Peter Nyama, a one-time Zimbabwean international. Another Zimbabwean, Roy Barreto, is currently (2002) coaching Stars.

Sundowns have also brought in their fair share: Ernest Chirwali and Cedric Nakhumuwa in the Eighties; and later Lovemore Chafunya, who was to make a name for himself as a goal-getter of high note.

The most recent big name was Raphael Chukwu, who now plies his trade with Bari in the Italian Serie B. Others include former Cameroon midfielder Roger Feutmba, and goal-keepers Nelson Bandura (from Zimbabwe) and Ronnie Kananelo (from Namibia).

Ted Dumitru, a former Swaziland national coach, helped give Chiefs their muscle in the 1980s with such signings as William "Cool Cat" Shongwe, and strikers Absalom "Scara" Thindwa and Abel Shongwe, whose performances on the field helped the Amakhosi claim a number of trophies.

Other players to have donned the Chiefs jersey over the years include former Malawian international Jack Chamangwane, Zairean (Congolese) goalkeeper Botende Eshele and, more recently, Namibian internationals Robert Nauseb and his cousin Mohammed Auseb.

Also well worth mentioning in the context of foreign talent are the Swallows trio of Mario Varaz, Eddie Campodonico and Raul Gonzalez, all from Chile, South America. They brought solid stability to their new squad. And then there is the Malawian Bennet Gondwe, who plied his trade in Durban, for Bush Bucks, in their Eighties halcyon days. Gondwe tormented defenders with his left foot, and within two years helped his team to both a league title and the JPS Series Cup. This was the time when Lawrence Ngubane was at his prime as manager of the all-conquering Durban side.

Significantly, the top goal-scorer since the formation of the Premier Soccer League has consistently been a foreign player – first Wilfred Mugeyi, then Raphael Chukwu, then Benjamin Mwaruwari, and most recently Gilbert Mushangazhike.

FRAUDS AND FALSE NAMES

Some clubs, in their anxiety to buy winning talent, registered their foreign players with fraudulent South African identity documents in order to overcome immigration regulations – a simple enough process, it seems, if we believe recent investigative reports.

Liberian goalkeeper Anthony Tokpah appeared as Anthony Aphane, a Northern Sotho (SePedi) name. Another Liberian, who arrived in this country on a Friday, was baptised Friday Roberts – Witbank Aces, who had been knocked out of the BobSave Superbowl by Manning Rangers (where Tokpah played then), helped police and local authorities unearth this scam. The two players were deported.

Ernest Chirwali, who is now known as Ernest Mtawali, was at the time of writing battling with Home Affairs authorities to prove the authenticity of his identification. He claims that he is now a bona fide South African as his mother was born in this country. He was brought in by Bloemfontein Celtic. Incidentally, Chirwali/Mtawali played in Europe under the name of Petrus Molemela. The grey-haired Bloemfontein Celtic boss who brought him to this country later became his father-in-law.

ABOVE *False colours – Bloemfontein Celtic's Liberian goalkeeper Anthony Topkah, seen clearing the ball from Andries Mpondo of Moroka Swallows, called himself Anthony Aphane, a local (SePedi) name.*

ABOVE *Absalom Thindwa rounds Arcadia Shepherds' midfielders. The former Swaziland international was highly rated locally.*

CHAPTER 14

BAFANA'S FIRST MOMENT OF GLORY

In 1991 "Stix" Morewa prophesied that the newly-liberated South African squad would win the African Cup of Nations, jewel in the continent's soccer crown. Less than six years later they did just that.

DEAFENING ROARS OF APPROVAL shook the foundations of Johannesburg's First National Bank (FNB) stadium when Nelson Mandela, South Africa's favourite son and until recently the world's most famous political prisoner, gingerly climbed the podium, right hand characteristically raised and wearing the No 9 jersey of the national soccer team – the same shirt number of South Africa's captain, Neil Tovey. It was a moment of triumph, a moment all South Africa had been waiting for since the de-restriction of the country's sport four years before.

Yes! Bafana Bafana had come of age! They were accepted as the African continent's best team – by virtue of winning the coveted African Cup of Nations.

START OF A DREAM

The vision of victory in the Cup of Nations started in 1991 when the South African Football Association (Safa) was formed. Solomon "Stix" Morewa, then secretary-general of the organisation, prophesied that the country would soon host the jewel in the African continent's soccer crown. Sceptics did not take him seriously.

Such hopes suffered a setback, and the sceptics were apparently proved right, when Bafana Bafana, in the first year or so, performed badly on the international scene.

Worse still, Jeff Butler, the first national coach, was fired before the team had even kicked a single ball in an international match.

ABOVE *South African statesman and football fan Nelson Mandela congratulates Edward Motale (left) and Linda Buthelezi.*
OPPOSITE *Bafana Bafana defender David Nyathi (right) cleans up from an Algerian opponent in the African Cup of Nations quarter-final match. South Africa won 2-1.*

His assistant, Stanley Tshabalala, assumed command, and took Bafana Bafana to their first official international match, against Zimbabwe in Harare. It was a disaster: the team suffered a humiliating 4-1 drubbing. This was followed by a 4-0 pasting by the Super Eagles of Nigeria and a same-score hiding by Mexico. A scornful public latched onto these scorelines and began calling the national team "the 4 x 4". The national squad also failed to qualify for the 1994 World Cup in the United States and, in the same year, for the African Cup of Nations finals in Tunisia.

It was such results that led soccer-lovers to look cynically at Morewa and, when he continued to insist that Safa fully intended South Africa to host the African Cup of Nations, to conclude that he had totally lost it. But they were wrong.

The turning point came with the appointment of Clive Barker as national coach in April 1994. Barker's first promise to the South[...]

African Football Association was that he would both win the 1996 Cup of Nations finals in Kenya and qualify for the 1998 World Cup finals in France.

BARKER BREAKS NEW GROUND

The new coach, a stocky man with knowledge, experience and drive, soon turned Bafana Bafana into a formidable side, as the initial qualifying results showed. The boys chalked up a 1-0 victory over Madagascar in Antananarivo, the Indian Ocean island's capital, and a similar win against Mauritius in Mmabatho. They then held the group favourites, Zambia, to a 1-1 draw in Lusaka.

As there were no more qualifiers to be played, Barker asked for friendly games to keep Bafana on their toes. He also suggested that a four-cornered tournament be arranged – a stroke of genius, since such a tournament would have an identical format as the opening round of the African Cup of Nations.

Bafana emerged the winners of the Four Nations tournament after drawing the first encounter (against Zambia) 2-2, going on to beat Egypt 2-0 and overcoming Zimbabwe 2-0 in the final game.

This was all excellent preparation for the big challenge ahead, and just the morale-boosting performance Barker needed.

The wily coach then asked for European opposition to test his team's strength, and Safa managed to secure a visit to South Africa by three-time world champions Germany.

The match between South Africa and Germany formed part of the official opening of the Johannesburg stadium. And what a game it turned out to be as Doctor Khumalo, a key member of the Barker squad, turned the German defence inside out. Newcomers Bafana held the disciplined German machine to a 0-0 draw.

A major disappointment hit the 1996 African Cup of Nations tournament when the defending

ABOVE *A watchful John Moshoeu, one of the stars of the tournament, looks out for a team-mate in Bafana's 1-0 victory over Mauritius.*

RIGHT *Doctor Khumalo congratulates Shaun Bartlett after the first of the latter's two goals against Malawi. South Africa won 3-0.*

ABOVE *Semi-final action – Ghana's Isaac Asare takes on John Moshoeu at Johannesburg's FNB stadium. The date: 31 January 1996.*

champions, Nigeria, withdrew following a row between the South African and Nigerian governments over political governance of the latter's country. The Super Eagles, who were already ensconced in their South African camp, pulled out despite efforts made to get the Nigerian authorities to change their stance. Nevertheless, Africa's premier tournament promised to be a great success: for the first time 16 countries were to take part. They were Algeria, Angola, Burkina Faso, Cameroon, Egypt, Gabon, Ghana, Ivory Coast, Liberia, Mozambique, Nigeria, Sierra Leone, South Africa, Tunisia, Zaire and Zambia.

South Africa was in Group A with Angola, Cameroon and Egypt. The four played their games at the FNB stadium in Johannesburg. Group B, based in Bloemfontein, consisted of

Algeria, Burkina Faso, Sierra Leone and Zambia. Group C, in Durban, comprised Gabon, Liberia and Zaire and the last group, D, in Port Elizabeth, featured Ghana, Ivory Coast, Mozambique and Tunisia.

OPENING SHOTS

Barker had then to face, as every coach must, perhaps his most difficult task – select his final squad of 22 players. Eventually he chose the following:

Goalkeepers: Andre Arendse (Cape Town Spurs), Roger De Sa (Mamelodi Sundowns) and John Tlale (Qwa Qwa Stars)

Defenders: Edward Motale (Orlando Pirates), Sizwe Motaung (Mamelodi Sundowns), David Nyathi (Cape Town Spurs), Lucas Radebe (Leeds United, England), Neil Tovey (Kaizer

ABOVE *Mark Fish was always solid in the South African defence, and staged effective counters from the back.*

RIGHT *Shaun Bartlett in action for Bafana in the African Cup of Nations final against Tunisia. South Africa won 2-0.*

OPPOSITE *Frank Amankwah, the Ghanaian midfielder, was regarded as the key player in his country's squad.*

Chiefs), Andrew Tucker (Pretoria City), Linda Buthelezi (Mamelodi Sundowns)

Linkmen: Doctor Khumalo (Kaizer Chiefs), August Makalakalane (FC Zurich, Switzerland), Helman Mkhalele (Orlando Pirates), John Moeti (Orlando Pirates), Zane Moosa (Mamelodi Sundowns), John Moshoeu (Kocaelispor, Turkey), Eric Tinkler (Victori Setubal, Portugal)

Strikers: Shaun Bartlett (Cape Town Spurs), Phil Masinga (Leeds United, England), Daniel Mudau (Mamelodi Sundowns) and Mark Williams (Wolverhampton Wanderers, England).

Barker then deployed experienced coaches to assess the other teams in the different venues and thus help him plan a winning strategy. Jomo Sono, who headed the technical committee, led the group.

On January 13 an estimated 75 000 spectators crammed into the FNB stadium to watch South Africa open their challenge for the trophy against Cameroon, a team deservedly known as the "Indomitable Lions". It was a Cameroon

fresh from a World Cup quarterfinal berth at Italia 90 and now, clearly, top dog in the African Nations Cup. But it took Phil Masinga a mere 14 minutes to find the back of the net and send the near capacity crowd into frenzy. Mark Williams scored the second in the 47th minute, and when John Moshoeu scored the third in the 55th, the Lions were forced to yield both the match and their reputation as Africa's finest. This sterling performance was followed by a hard-fought 1-0 victory over Angola, the goal coming from Williams in the 57th minute.

Four days later, in the third game, South Africa met Egypt – a team still smarting from their 2-0 defeat during the Simba Four Nations tournament played the previous December. And the Egyptians got their revenge when Ahmed el Kass found the net as early as the seventh minute. This was going to be the score-line at the end of the 90 minutes. Bafana had suffered their first defeat of the tournament.

But Clive Barker remained positive, even optimistic. "Defeat has been a blessing in disguise," he said. "The boys were becoming a bit complacent. We needed this as a wake-up call." South Africa and Egypt went through to the next round. The two had finished with the same number of points but a superior goal difference gave Bafana the homeground advantage: they would continue to play their games at the FNB stadium in Johannesburg.

South Africa faced Algeria in the knockout stage of the tournament – another tough encounter. And indeed the Algerians proved stubborn, but they finally cracked in the 72nd minute when Mark Fish made a darting run from the centre of defence and eventually, to a roar from the stadium's packed terraces, finished off the move he had started. The crowd fell quiet when Tarek Lazizi equalised in the 84th minute but the silence was short-lived as yet another hero of the tournament, John "Shoes" Moshoeu, quickly replied to give the South Africans the edge.

Beating Algeria put Bafana into the semi-final, against the Black Stars of Ghana. The West African country, the last hurdle between the host team and the final, had demolished all opposition on their way to the crucial match, and they were the only country to have won the tournament a total of four times. But they had come up for some rough treatment at the hands of Zaire (which prompted their coach, Ismael Kutz, to complain that "Zaire did not come to play"). Ghanaian star Abedi Pele Ayew had picked up an ankle injury after being hacked by Nzelo Lembi, who'd been awarded a red card for his troubles. All this was to blunt Ghana's capability somewhat.

TRIUMPH AT FNB

Wednesday, January 31, 1996, will go down in soccer history books as the day that South Africa – Bafana Bafana – dished out one of their best performances on a football field, if not *the* best. A lot of planning went into the game. Doctor Khumalo once told me that Jomo Sono gave them a very tough talk in the dressing room before the kick-off, and suggested Khumalo be played on the left flank. Sono said that right back Frank Amankwah was the engine of the Ghanaian team. Close down Amankwah, he said, and you've closed down Ghana. Khumalo

CAF African Cup of Nations 1996 – Finals

South Africa qualified as hosts

STANDINGS: *Group stage*

	PLAYED	WON	DRAWN	LOST	FOR	AGAINST	POINTS
South Africa	3	2	0	1	4	1	6
Egypt	3	2	0	1	3	1	6
Cameroon	3	1	1	1	5	7	4
Angola	3	0	1	2	4	6	1

Match details

All matches played at Soccer City, Johannesburg

Finals, Group A. January 13. **Bafana Bafana. 3 – Cameroon 0**. Bafana goals: Phil Masinga (14), Mark Williams (37), John Moshoeu (55). Attendance: 75 000.

Finals, Group A. January 20. **Bafana Bafana 1 – Angola 0**. Bafana goal: Mark Williams (57). Attendance: 40 000.

Finals, Group A. January 24. **Bafana Bafana 0 – Egypt 1**. Egypt goal: El Kass (7). Attendance: 20 000.

Quarter-final. January 27. **Bafana Bafana 2 – Algeria 1**. Bafana goals: Mark Fish (72), John Moshoeu (85), Algeria goal Lazizi (84). Attendance: 50 000.

Semi-final. January 31. **Bafana Bafana 3 – Ghana 0**. Bafana goals: John Moshoeu (22, 87), Shaun Bartlett (46). Attendance: 75 000.

Final. February 3. **Bafana Bafana 2 – Tunisia 0**. Bafana goals: Mark Williams (72, 74). Attendance: 75 000.

GROUP 3: *Key Players*

Doctor Khumalo The cog that kept the engine room (the midfield) together throughout. The video of the highlights reveals that he had a hand in nearly every goal Bafana scored in the tournament.

Mark Williams Ended as one of the tournament's leading scorers. Williams came late into the match, and in the final he found the net twice to secure victory for South Africa.

Andre Arendse Goalkeeper, who had not conceded a goal for several matches. He proved to be the backbone of the team – all the players had supreme confidence in their last line of defence.

Neil Tovey Captained the team with distinction, and his reading of the game was superb. He anticipated moves before they became dangerous, was always there to uplift his troops when they needed encouragement. Deservedly, it was Tovey who lifted the African Unity trophy high at the end of the tournament.

John Moshoeu One of the mainstays of the side in midfield. His sleek ball skills were marvellous to watch, and he was the one player who added moments of real brilliance to the tournament.

Lucas Radebe One of the miracles of modern medicine was that Radebe actually played: he had suffered a career threatening injury and was initially ruled out. He turned out to be one of the stars of the tournament.

ABOVE *The last battle – Tunisia's defence and keeper are caught on the wrong foot by an opening header from Mark Williams (obscured).*

was instructed always to take the ball to the stocky defender. Keep him back-pedalling. Don't allow him any chance to launch an attack.

Bafana went ahead as early as the 22nd minute when Shoes Moshoeu found the net – a goal that gave the local team the psychological as well as the scoreline edge going into the second half. And then, just 20 seconds after the interval, Shaun Bartlett took the sails off the Black Stars with another goal, and Moshoeu completed his brace with three minutes of play remaining to give the squad an emphatic 3-0 victory over the West African soccer giants.

On February 3, 1996, a glorious Saturday afternoon, an estimated record-breaking crowd of 110 000 people gathered at the FNB stadium to watch Bafana Bafana appear in their first ever African Cup of Nations final – against Tunisia. The weather was kind. Political heavyweights present ranged from then President Nelson Mandela to the Zulu King, Goodwill Zwelithini. So was F.W. de Klerk, the last white president of this country. Other notables included the late Steve Tshwete, then minister of sport, and the then Gauteng provincial premier, Tokyo Sexwale. Referee Charles Masembe of Uganda

was in charge of the epic battle; everybody agreed that he was just the right choice.

The game began with the two sides sizing each other up. Medhi Ben Slimane, the speedy forward, then started carving holes in the Bafana Bafana defence. He troubled Lucas Radebe and Mark Fish with his pace – but by the end of the first stanza, there were still no goals. In the 65th minute Barker introduced Williams and Philemon Masinga.

Williams was on the field for just seven minutes when he majestically rose above the confused Tunisians to nod home South Africa's opening goal. This sent the largely South African crowd into frenzy. Two minutes later, Doctor Khumalo intercepted a pass in midfield and sent a typical defence-splitting pass on to Williams. Chokri el Ouaer tried to close the angle, but Williams angled his ground shot around the keeper and found the back of the net. Every man, woman and child in the FNB shouted his or her voice hoarse in celebration.

Not a single soul left the packed stadium at the end of the ninety minutes. Everybody wanted to savour South Africa's moment of triumph at the 20th African Cup of Nations.

ABOVE *We are the champions! South African state president Nelson Mandela joyfully raises his arms as Bafana Bafana captain Neil Tovey hoists aloft the African Cup of Nations trophy.*

CHAPTER 15

THE ROAD TO FRANCE '98

A magnificent Phil Masinga goal catapulted Bafana on their march to the finals of their first World Cup – a march along a route lined with some exhilarating qualifying matches.

WHENEVER FOOTBALL TALK turns to South Africa's inaugural challenge for the World Cup, "that goal" is mentioned.

The 1998 World Cup was Bafana Bafana's first opportunity to pit themselves against the best in global soccer. After failing to make the trip to the USA for the 1994 Cup, they just had to go to France. Something to do with national pride.

They needed a draw – at home, against the team from the People's Republic of Congo (sometimes called Congo Brazzaville) – to qualify for their first real venture into the most prestigious soccer competition of all. An estimated crowd of 90 000 gathered in the FNB stadium; millions more watched on television and listened on radio. The hour of reckoning had dawned for the national side. Would Bafana's opponents halt their march to Paris? Or would they get there by sharing the spoils? Better still, would they go to the games in grand style with a resounding win?

There was a huge police presence at the FNB, a reminder of the intense hostility between Bafana and Congo. Bafana had, controversially, lost the first-leg encounter 2-0 away at Pointe Noire – literally at the point of bayonets. Soldiers had abused the South

ABOVE *"Siyaya" – coach Clive Barker spreads wings in his famous "take-off" celebration after Phil Masinga's magic goal against Congo.*
OPPOSITE *David Nyathi closes down Nigerian striker Rachidi Yikeni in a World Cup qualifier in Johannesburg. The teams played to a goalless draw.*

Africans and the game itself left much to be desired. This is material for another story; but suffice to say that the treatment meted out to Bafana was still fresh in the fans' memories. Safa called in the police (they feared a repeat of the 1995 incident, when Orlando Pirates supporters forced fans of the Ivory Coast side, Asec Mimosas, to jump into the moat surrounding the pitch).

Bafana started the game gingerly and looked somewhat anxious in their play. Congo were the first to threaten, with Machembe Younga-Mouhani, their two-goal hero in the Pointe Noire victory, beating Mark Fish on the left flank only for his cross to be wasted. As the game progressed, so did the tension grow. Then, in the 14th minute, Congo's Brice Mokossi attempted a pass near the centre-line inside his own half; Doctor Khumalo stretched out his leg, intercepted, and sent a deadly pinpoint pass to a teammate; Phil Masinga pushed the ball once, looked up, and – with the Congolese defenders expecting him to advance further – unleashed a thunderous right-footed shot that went over the goalkeeper into the roof of the net. That goal!

The FNB crowd went berserk. Coach Clive Barker leaped into his famous celebratory aeroplane take-off. Masinga ran towards the goal, turned his jersey back-to-front and proudly pointed to the number 6 and his surname.

With the game still that young, no one imagined that that would be the goal to take South Africa to France. Resolute (if not often lucky) defending ensured that it would, and when Charles Massembe blew the final whistle, pandemonium erupted in the

RIGHT *Premature departure – Bafana defender Mark Fish, with a concerned Danny Jordaan behind him, leaves the field bleeding from a deliberate elbowing by Congo's Richard Akiana.*

BELOW *Shaun Bartlett deftly avoids a tackle in the World Cup qualifier against Malawi. Bafana won 1-0.*

FNB stadium. The triumphant team did a lap of honour; many of the players shed tears of joy and pride.

In the post-match interviews, Masinga described the goal as one "I'll remember for the rest of my life".

Bafana then went on to France – to complete a journey that had started in Blantyre two years earlier, on June 1, 1996.

THE RUN-UP TO THE CUP

In the preliminary, elimination stages of the World Cup, South Africa was pitted against Southern African neighbours Malawi, and Bafana's winning margin should have been much more than the 1-0 that appeared on the final scoreboard. But the victory sent the country into the second round – a home game against the same opponents – and the squad were confident of success. This they soon ensured at a sparsely populated FNB stadium. Shaun Bartlett scored the first goal with the game only five minutes old. Fish made it 2-0 on 39 minutes and Bartlett repaid Barker's faith in him by completing his brace two minutes' later.

The country then waited for the group qualifiers, and everyone was delighted when Bafana were seeded, which meant they would not be matched against the likes of Nigeria (who had humiliated them 4-0 in the fight for places at USA '94). And with powerhouses Cameroon, Egypt and Morocco also among the seeds, the country's soccer fraternity boldly declared "Siyaya eFrance – We are going to France."

The draw itself, conducted at Fifa's head offices in Zurich, placed Bafana in the same group with Republic of Congo (Brazzaville), Zaire (later renamed Democratic Republic of Congo) and Zambia.

Zaire were the first opponents, and Bafana duly registered their first maximum points.

After the Zaire victory, it was off to the Copperbelt for a clash with the Zambians. Zambia had lost their opening game 1-0 to the Congo and many thought Bafana would have no problem gaining their second maximum tally. The Zambian media, for their part, confidently predicted a mauling for Bafana – and in front of a capacity 35 000 crowd, in hot and humid conditions, the two battled to a creditable goalless draw. After the game Barker boldly declared his side was just one victory away from participating in the World Cup finals.

"Our next game match against Congo in Pointe-Noire will be crucial. If we collect three points I reckon we can book our places to France," Barker said. "The Dog" (Barker's nick name), however, warned against getting carried away. "There's still a lot of work to be done", he added. The warning was well justified. As we've seen, Bafana became badly unstuck in Pointe Noire.

The 2-0 loss, marred as it was by the unsporting behaviour (on and off the pitch) of the Congolese, sent Bafana tumbling down to earth. The prophets of doom were quick to declare that yet another South African World Cup dream had bitten the dust.

Still, Barker and his boys remained positive, sure that they would be joining 31 of the world's top footballing countries in France for the month-long tournament. Having watched Zaire draw 2-2 with Zambia in their qualifying match (played in neutral Zimbabwe, due to the civil strife in Zaire) the coach declared South Africa was still very much in the running. "To qualify we have to get a point off Zaire and gamble on winning both our home matches against Zambia and Congo," he said.

He added that he did not mind where they played (the venue for the match yet to be decided) and that his "main care is that I know what we have to do to go to France".

Fifa chose Lome, capital of the West African state of Togo, as the venue, and such was Bafana's popularity that on the day of the match, April 27 – coincidentally, South Africa's Freedom Day – that they seemed to enjoy more support than the local team, many Togolese

World Cup 1998

Hosts: France

QUALIFYING ROUNDS: *Final Standings*

	PLAYED	WON	DRAWN	LOST	FOR	AGAINST	POINTS
South Africa	6	4	1	1	7	3	13
Congo Rep	6	3	1	2	5	5	10
Zambia	6	2	2	2	7	6	8
Zaire (DR Congo)	6	0	2	2	4	9	4

FINALS: *Group C match reports*

Bafana Bafana 0 – France 3. June 12, Velodrome Stadium, Marseille. Attendance 60 000. France goals: Dugarry (34), Pierre Issa (own goal, 77), Henry (89). Bafana showed a degree of determination, but tended to lose both concentration and co-ordination, and their tactical game couldn't match the more experienced (and more skillful) French. Shooting was poor, there was unnecessary dribbling, and support from midfield and defence tended to be slow. Outstanding players: David Nyathi, Mark Fish, Quinton Fortune.

Bafana Bafana 1 – Denmark 1. June 18. Municipal Stadium, Toulouse. Attendance 33 300. Bafana goal: Benedict McCarthy (52); Denmark goal: Nielsen (13). This was South Africa's first point in World Cup history. The team showed much more discipline and fighting spirit, and there was a good combination of zone and man-to-man marking. Excellent individual technique in defence. Midfield playmaker: John Moshoeu. Colombian referee sent off three players (Molnar 67, Alfred Phiri 69, Wieghorst 85). Outstanding players: Moshoeu, McCarthy.

Bafana Bafana 2 – Saudi Arabia 2. June 24, Parc Lescure Stadium, Bordeaux. Attendance 35 000. Bafana goals: Shaun Bartlett (19, 89 pen); Saudi goals: Al Jaber (44 pen), Al Tunian (74 pen). The speed and skill of the strikers, and the execution of corners and set pieces, were Bafana's strong points. Midfield did not give good support to defence; good short passes in building up attacks, but element of surprise was missing. Outstanding players: Benedict McCarthy, Shaun Bartlett.

KEY PLAYERS

Benedict McCarthy Scored Bafana's first goal at a World Cup finals, a strike that went through the legs of Danish (and Manchester United) keeper Peter Schmeichel, who was rated best in the world at the time. Ball skills and anticipation outstanding.

Quinton Fortune Fully justified coach Phillippe Troussier's confidence, invariably playing a blinder in midfield. Unlucky to have a powerful shot come off the crossbar in the Denmark game – it would have been the winner.

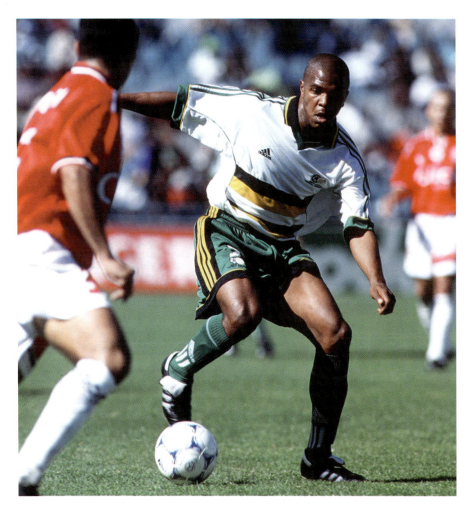

ABOVE *The good form continues – Quinton Fortune takes on a defender in Bafana's 2-1 victory over Egypt a few months after the World Cup.*

RIGHT *Benni McCarthy lifts his arms in celebration of a goal against Egypt.*

OPPOSITE CLOCKWISE FROM TOP LEFT *Happy hug: Phil Masinga and John Moshoeu after Bafana Bafana's World Cup qualifier victory against Congo in 1997; Shaun Bartlett is chaired off the pitch; Doctor Khumalo wings his way across the field after the Congo decider.*

bringing along posters of Nelson Mandela to show who they truly backed in the encounter. Which is not to say that the support was overwhelming – indeed the crowd numbered a poor 7 000, probably the smallest Bafana have ever played in front of. The coach left out captain Neil Tovey from the starting line-up, giving the skipper's armband instead to Lucas Radebe.

Khumalo opened the scoring after being set up by Brendan Augustine; Zaire equalised just four minutes later and then, late in the game, Khumalo and Masinga combined to carve out a memorable goal – Khumalo floated a beautiful, inch-perfect cross into the danger area, and the lanky striker rose majestically to nod the ball into the net. Masinga cramped a few minutes later and was forced to make way for Shaun Bartlett. But "Chippa" (as Masinga is affectionately known), with his tenth goal for Bafana, had already done the job for his country.

South Africa was now level with Congo (which

lost 3-0 away to Zambia) but the Congolese had a better goal difference. Bafana were left with two home matches to complete their campaign – and the road ahead looked rosy.

The game against Zambia was the clincher, Bafana recording their biggest win to date: they hammered in three without reply. When the final whistle blew Barker hurled his T-shirt into the crowd, described the game as "fantastic" and even in his jubilation was still full of praise for the Zambians, who went into the match ranked number one on the continent: "They are terrific footballers," he said. "It's just that we were better on the day."

Before the Congo decider, Bafana – who had Sundowns' Isaac Shai as the only newcomer to the squad – played a Free State Select XI and managed just a 1-0 win, courtesy of a Doctor Khumalo penalty. And immediately, doubts abounded and many questioned how a side that fails to hammer a local pick-up team would perform against a national squad. German-born Horst Kriete, who occupied the directorship position for Safa's coaching department, offered words of advice some days before the match: "We must dictate the pace against Congo.

ABOVE *Phil Masinga sprints through the Congo's defence in the crucial qualifier.*

Concentration on the field is going to be very crucial. We have to be mentally tuned in on the game. If we play to our potential we will not be stopped on our march to France."

Then State President Nelson Mandela sent the team a message of encouragement that read: "Tomorrow's contest is a celebration of the achievements of the South African people. I am looking forward to a mighty display of all the beautiful colours of our rainbow nation. I also welcome our brothers from the Republic of Congo in our society and assure them of our

people's hospitality. Saturday will produce a good result, and that should take us to France."

It is now history that, 14 minutes into the game, Masinga scored "that goal" – the goal that sent them to France.

THE BIG CUP LET-DOWN

Of course, just getting to the World Cup finals was a major victory for a soccer brotherhood that had been isolated for so many years. And the journey had been full of excitement and fine football. But once in France, facing the world's best, Bafana failed to deliver – perhaps understandably.

In their first match, played against the host country in Marseille on June 12, 1998, in front of a partisan, wildly cheering, 60 000-strong crowd, the South Africans conceded three goals without reply. It was a champagne performance by France, fully worthy of the eventual Cup winners. Stars of the show were Christophe Dugarry and Zinedine Zidane, who stamped his authority on the match from the first whistle. Bafana seemed flat, unable to cope with the relentless French attacks; said Mark Fish afterwards: "We just have to play our natural way, the way that got us to the World Cup. We cannot defend for 90 minutes."

Denmark, Bafana's next opponents, proved a lot less dominant in a game notable for (and spoiled by) the number of cards handed out by Colombian referee John Jairo Toro – three reds and seven yellows!

The match was played in Toulouse on June 18, and the end result was an inconclusive 1-1 draw, which gave Denmark four points and moved them within sight of the second round. Benni McCarthy scored Bafana Bafana's goal, the country's first ever in a World Cup, after a clever back-heel pass from Shaun Bartlett, but all in all it had been a disappointing game, marred by the number of fouls in the second half.

Bafana could still qualify, just, if they beat minnows Saudi Arabia in their third match, and if France hammered Denmark in the other group game. But they could only manage another draw (2-2). Both South African goals were scored by Bartlett; both Saudi goals came from questionable penalties, and both involved defender Pierre Issa. Coach Philippe Troussier, commenting on his team's overall performance, said that Bafana's inexperience had showed during the tournament, that the players lacked mental toughness, and that he "never really felt that there was that collective commitment on the part of everyone".

That soon changed. The national squad had shown real commitment in the lead-up to the Cup, had lost it for a moment in France, but was to regain its will to win in the years to come.

ABOVE *Bafana earn a creditable draw (1-1) against Denmark in Toulouse to give South Africa their first point in a World Cup. Pictured in action is Alfred Phiri.*

CHAPTER 16

THE GREAT WORLD CUP ROBBERY

South Africa's bid was strong; promises had been made, and Fifa had the perfect opportunity to level the grossly uneven playing field. But in the end it was betrayal, not fairness, that won the day.

TO SOUTH AFRICAN SOCCER-LOVERS, New Zealander Charles Dempsey is Enemy Number One. On Thursday July 6, 2000, he defied the instructions of his federation to vote for South Africa and, instead, abstained. This gave Germany the lone vote that enabled it to host the 2006 World Cup. The voting was conducted in Zurich, the Swiss capital and home to Fifa, the world body that controls soccer. The countries bidding for the honour of hosting the World Cup were Brazil (South America), England, Germany (both Europe), Morocco and South Africa (both Africa).

Brazil had withdrawn from the race – courtesy of a gentleman's agreement with South Africa. "Support us for 2006 and if we win we will support you for 2010," was what Danny Jordaan, chief executive of the South African bid committee, had told the Brazilians.

The English bid was doomed from day one, since years before England had asked Germany to withdraw from competing to host the 1996 European Championship, in return for which the English would give their full support to the Germans for the 2006 World Cup. The English failed to keep their promise and threw in their own bid for the 2006 Cup – in the event a stillborn bid: the other European nations were dead set against it from the start. Morocco,

in their third attempt to bring the World Cup to Africa for the first time, stood little if any chance at all. The North Africans hadn't even started building the stadiums they would need.

And South Africa?

We thought we had it all. Though FNB stadium in Johannesburg remains South Africa's only world-class soccer venue, the relationship between the South African Football Association and the South African Rugby Football Union meant that more than enough rugby stadiums of international standard would be available. That's exactly what happened when South Africa successfully hosted, and won, the 1996 African Cup of Nations.

Of the six Fifa confederations, only Africa and Oceana had never hosted the World Cup. The situation presented Fifa with a perfect platform to end Europe's stranglehold on the event, a splendid opportunity for the parliament of world football to level the grossly uneven playing field. The football federation's challenge was to demonstrate to the world that none of its six continental confederations – Africa, Asia, South America, North and Central America, Oceana and Europe – was more equal than the others.

CAF, the African confederation, boasts the highest number of affiliates but has never been allowed to host soccer's greatest spectacle. The so-called Dark Continent remained (and still remains) the odd man out despite its growing stature in world football over recent years. How apt then was South Africa's rallying call for the bid? It was Africa's turn.

But it was not to be.

ABOVE *Primary school children demonstrate in the streets of Lenasia, near Johannesburg, in support of the country's World Cup 2006 bid.* OPPOSITE *South Africa has world class sporting facilities, many of the bigger and better ones dual-purpose stadiums.*

ABOVE *Irvin Khoza – led the delegation that mounted a campaign for the 2006 World Cup.*

ABOVE *CAF president Issa Hayatou – strongly supported South Africa as the host of choice.*

ABOVE *Franz Beckenbauer – orchestrated Germany's campaign to stage soccer's premier event.*

DANNY REMEMBERS

South Africa's bid was solid as a rock, or so it seemed. But Germany came out triumphant, winning the race with a 12-11 vote-count – thanks to Dempsey.

Dempsey undid a South African dream that had started in Ouagadougou, Burkina Faso, in 1998 and which, after three years of globetrotting, lobbying and canvassing support for its translation into reality, died a sudden death.

With the dream went the 130 000 jobs that would have been created if the World Cup had been played in South Africa, together with other, massive, economic spin-offs – currently, the total revenue of the World Cup hovers around the $30-billion mark.

No one is better qualified to relive the painful demise of South Africa's hopes than Danny Jordaan, chief executive of South Africa's ill-fated bid. "The weekend before the decision on the host country," he remembers, "I was in England watching the Euro 2000 final between France and Italy at the invitation of Uefa. We were seated together with Franz Beckenbaur and Fedor Radmann, the leaders of the German bid. Bobby Charlton, who was heading the English bid, was sitting just behind me.

"Radmann said he recognised that we had a strong bid. He asked that we withdraw from the race and said Germany would support us for the 2010 bid instead. I told him that we were confident of our position and withdrawal was out of the equation. He said it was just a pity that Fifa had to chose between two strong candidatures."

This was in contrast to Fifa's options in the two previous Cup spectacles: in 1994, the race was between Switzerland, Morocco and the US, and predictably the land of the Stars and Stripes scooped the reward. France and Morocco were in the running for the rights to host the 1998 tournament and, again unsurprisingly, the French beat the North Africans to the winning tape. Logically, Japan and South Korea got the 2002 event, the first for Asia and the first co-hosted World Cup.

"Our arrangement with Brazil threw the Germans into a complete spin," says Jordaan. "To say they were shocked would be an understatement." Franz Beckenbaur, who was heading the German bid, blasted it as underhand. But who cared? To make sure that no stone was left unturned, the CAF delegation met Dempsey to remind him of his obligations.

Unexpectedly, Dempsey pleaded ignorance of the mandate he had been given by his confederation – of the instruction to vote for South Africa if England bombed out of contention. Recalls Jordaan: "He said he was not compelled to vote for South Africa, claiming he had a free vote. We called his federation and asked for the minutes of the meeting where he was given the mandate to vote for us. We got the minutes, showed them to him and he said: 'Oh, yes!' So whatever permutation you looked at, South Africa was a strong candidate, and we consolidated our position ahead of the final run in."

The only option open to the Germans was to work on the Asians, and on Dempsey. South Africa was confident the Asians would stand with the Africans, as has been tradition over the decades. The confidence stemmed from the strong Afro-Asia ties between the two continents. For decades they had been brothers-in-arms in the struggle against colonialism.

Then, lo and behold, the unthinkable happened! South Africa got not a single vote from Asia. Dempsey banged in the final nail, and the dream was shattered.

"The memories and the experience of our apartheid past came flooding back," Jordaan explains. "It exposed the power relations in Fifa. The inequality and the imbalances in terms of power between Europe and the rest of the other continents in Fifa came to the fore, in stark contrast with the spirit of fair play in the Fifa Family."

Europeans constitute three of every five who serve on Fifa's sub-committees. "That is the reality of Fifa," Jordaan goes on. "Our bid process moved us to highlight that Fifa had to move to a situation where its structural, philosophical and ideological position has to be more in sync with representivity, justice and fair play."

As for Dempsey's betrayal, Jordaan's feelings move from disgust to bemusement. "It's funny that it was Africa that fought to ensure that Oceana became a fully-fledged member of the Fifa fold," he says. "We bailed them out as their acceptance faced resistance from other quarters. But when the first time came for them to use their vote, Dempsey did us dirty."

SA SOLDIERS ON

Despite the deep disappointment, South Africa picked themselves up and dusted themselves off. They were bruised but not broken. Yes, we are going for Round Two. The same men who were entrusted with the responsibility to lead the abortive bid, Jordaan and Irvin Khoza (vice-president of Safa), will assume the duties of, respectively, chairman and chief executive officer for the 2010 bid – as they had done in 2000.

Lessons were learned in 2000; friendships were forged, South Africa will go for the second bite of the cherry wiser than before. They are no longer wet behind the ears in the bidding business: the path has been travelled before and this time it must be negotiated more carefully as we have now learnt that it is a minefield. "Furthermore," writes Fifa supremo Seth Blatter, "with its strong bid to host the 2006 World Cup, the South African FA gained a great deal of respect and recognition. These achievements showed that, in spite of international boycott, football has always thrived in South Africa, and it has now finally regained the opportunity to test itself on the world stage."

Fifa's recently announced rotational system for hosting the World Cup has prompted immense excitement around the African continent.

South Africans believe it's now their turn. That the bid came so close against such a rich and powerful footballing nation as Germany demonstrates the quality of the presentation – and that presentation is now even better. Add to that the fact that Fifa president Sepp Blatter threw his weight behind South Africa for 2006, and that South Africa voted to keep him in office, and there's every chance that the 2010 Cup will come to the southern tip of Africa. Top local companies are backing the campaign, and as mentioned, the experienced Khoza and Jordaan are in charge.

The only obstacle would be a decision by the North African countries – Morocco, Egypt, Tunisia, Libya – to put in a strong bid to co-host soccer's premier competition.

ABOVE *Next question? Danny Jordaan, chief executive of SAFA, headed the 2006 World Cup bid*

LEFT *The South African delegation receives a sympathetic welcome on its return from Europe.*

CHAPTER 17

BANYANA BANYANA HIT THE SCENE

Women's soccer, so long ignored in South Africa, was introduced to the wider public in highly dramatic fashion – by a combination of unruly spectators and television cameras.

SOUTH AFRICANS WITNESSED an unprecedented spectacle when the national women's team, Banyana Banyana, faced Nigeria in the final of the Second African Women's Championship at Vosloorus. On that November afternoon in 2000, fans jostled into the tiny stadium east of Johannesburg, packing it to the brim.

The South African side had already garnered huge support after their exploits were televised live. Admittance to the stadium was also free, and supporters who had already seen the trailblazing team in previous games (in which they had beaten Reunion 3-0, Uganda 3-0, Zimbabwe 2-1 and Ghana 1-0) were eager for action. Some of the more enterprising ones climbed onto the close-by pylons to get a bird's eye view of proceedings, while others perched precariously on the roof of the stadium's changing rooms.

It was an unforgettable day in many ways.

Coached by Fran Hilton-Smith, with Shakes Mashaba as technical adviser, Banyana stalwarts such as 39-year-old captain Desiree Ellis, midfielder Anna Monate, and defender Sibongile Khumalo had rarely been seen in action despite serving their country with distinction for several years. They were now able to showcase their talents on a national scale for the first time. So were an impressive number of rising stars such as strikers Jo-Anne Solomon and Portia Modise, midfielder Veronica Phewa, and defenders Maud Khumalo and Evah Mokwape.

Then, to the embarrassment of all South Africa, unruly elements in the crowd – troublesome characters who were unable to accept Nigeria's two-goal lead – pelted the players with missiles, forcing officials to abandon the game.

OPPOSITE *Banyana Banyana's Thsepiso Masenimela tussles with Nigeria's Nkechi Egbe. The game, although spoilt by crowd misbehaviour, showed that women's soccer was here to stay.*

The unsavoury incident, watched live on television, was condemned by the country's elite. Behind the scenes, however, it was agreed that the tournament had succeeded in introducing, in no uncertain fashion, women's soccer to the wider public.

THE BATTLE FOR RECOGNITION

The mood in the squad, and among those who watched, was a far cry from that of a few years before, when disenchanted players and a largely all-female technical staff toiled to get recognition from the national controlling body – the South African Football Association (Safa) – and exposure to a wider audience. At that time, and for years afterwards, women's soccer received minimal attention. The predominantly male authorities preferred devoting time and money to Bafana Bafana and AmaGlug-Glug, the under-23s.

Such was the frustration of the women that, not long before the championship, Ellis quit in disgust. She was fed up that players like her, who had committed themselves unselfishly to the game for several years, were being treated like third-rate citizens. However, after much persuasion, from both teammates and soccer fans, Ellis changed her mind and took part in the contest.

But some of the problems that beset Banyana then are still plaguing the game today.

THE FIRST MATCHES

South Africa were formally admitted to international women's soccer at Fifa's first Women's World Conference on Football in Switzerland in October 1992. The national squad was formed a year later and played their first game against Swaziland – and beat them 14-0! Male coach and former England player Terry Paine had mentored the side (the reluctance to appoint full-time coaching staff lasted for years).

A scatter of other friendly games followed, among them two in

Harare – the team beating Zimbabwe 2-1 and 8-0 in their opponents' own backyard.

In November 1994, after a year of inactivity, a side was quickly assembled for the African World Cup qualifiers. In their first-leg game, and with coach Sandile Bali at the helm, they beat Zambia. The game was played as a curtain-raiser to an under-23 match at Milpark; South Africa went on to thrash Zambia 6-2 in the second leg, played in Lusaka; beat Angola 3-1 at the Rand stadium; drew the return match in Luanda (despite playing on a pitch with grass ankle-length high), and finally succumbed, at the last hurdle, to Nigeria in March 1995, loosing 4-1 in Ibadan and 7-1 in Johannesburg. Nigeria went on to become Africa's sole representative at the Second Women's World Cup in Sweden that same year.

There followed another drought period – two years of inactivity – before Banyana played a solitary friendly against, and beat, Zimbabwe at FNB stadium in Johannesburg in June 1997. The game was the curtain-raiser to a Bafana friendly against Holland. Andries Maseko was the coach. It was a laudable victory, yet small consolation for a team which was hungry for success but which Safa was denying the opportunity to shine.

TAKING SOLID SHAPE

Banyana represented something new to the less privileged members of South African society, but women's soccer was not new in the country – it went back to the 1960s, and was played under the auspices of the South African Women's Football Association, which was affiliated to the Confederation of South African Sport. The first black players emerged at an inter-provincial tournament staged in Pretoria in 1979 – as did Ellis, one of several "coloured" people already involved in the game.

Multi-racial matches were staged in the townships from the late 1980s, and such was the enthusiasm for this branch of the game that the

LEFT *Gloria Hlalele, the skilful midfielder and star of the early days of Banyana Banyana.*

then Southern Transvaal association asked to enter three teams in the September 1993 inter-provincial tournament in Durban. And it was there that the likes of Gloria Hlalele, Fikile Sithole and Khabo Zitha showed they had as much skill and style as their male counterparts.

The national women's team failed to qualify for the 1998 World Cup, following which Safa formed a women's steering committee chaired by Nastasia Tsichlas, managing director of the Sundowns club. But the "Iron Lady", as she is popularly known, later resigned – although she publicly refused to disclose her reasons she was thought to have been disillusioned with Safa's perceived unwillingness to take the women's game seriously. The committee was then co-chaired by Ria Ledwaba, founder and owner of

the now-defunct Premier Soccer League club Ria Stars, and Kedi Tshoma, a top sports official and ardent campaigner for women's rights in sport dating back to the days of the former National Sports Council.

Fran Hilton-Smith, who had relentlessly fought for the recognition of women's soccer over many years, was sidelined, and women's soccer, for a time, went into disarray. But Hilton-Smith soldiered on, working tirelessly (for no pay), and was ultimately appointed (by Safa) full-time manager/caretaker coach of all women's national teams in 1999. Under her guidance, women's soccer took a giant step forward. Regular training camps were held; more frequent senior provincial and international matches were staged.

BELOW *Khabo Zitha (left) competes for the ball in Banyana's 1997 women's international against Zimbabwe.*

ABOVE *"Iron lady" Natasha Tsichlas pushed hard for the recognition of women's football*

With a technical team headed by Hilton-Smith and physiotherapist Caren Fleishman – later beefed up by doctor Dimikatso Ramagole and psychologist Nomsa Nkuna – the national team began to take solid shape.

FAILURE IN NIGERIA

Banyana Banyana was born in 1998, the players themselves choosing the name to reflect the image of success projected by their male counterparts, Bafana Bafana, who had won the 1996 African Cup of Nations.

As mentioned, the squad participated for the first time in the African Women's Championships in Nigeria in 1998, but were knocked out in the first round after being beaten 4-0 by Ghana and 3-2 by Cameroon. For the first time, two African teams – Nigeria and Ghana – then went on to represent the continent at the Women's World Cup in the United States the following year.

Nomalungelo Mooi coached the side in the African championships – one of only two women ever to do so – but the odds for success were stacked heavily against her because of dubious refereeing decisions.

The Ghana game in particular was played in the most comical of circumstances as players were forced to wade through water on the pitch after a major rain downfall. Field markings were virtually washed away. Despite several protests by the South Africans, match officials insisted the game had to go on.

The failure in Nigeria marked a turning point. A deeply disappointed Safa convened a women's football indaba in 1999; delegates drew up a blueprint that charted the way forward and charted, especially, preparations for the African Women's Championships to be staged near Johannesburg in November 2000.

The championships were a great marketing success (with the sole though major exception of crowd misbehaviour). All Banyana's games were televised, top female players showed off their skills and developed a cult following. Such was the team's technical deftness, that some fans thought they were more skilled than Bafana – an observation Safa did not take kindly to. The success of the occasion, moreover, further served to enhance the growing popularity for women's soccer world wide, prompting the Fifa president, Sepp Blatter, to comment that the future of soccer was indeed feminine.

BANYANA GETS BUSY

In July 2001 the inaugural Sanlam Halala Cup league – bankrolled to the tune of R15-million for three years by the leading insurance company – was launched. Over 300 teams from 25 Safa regions entered the tournament, which kicked off in September. Sanlam's investment did a great deal for the popularity of women's soccer.

Teams that had never been heard of came out of the woods to compete for national honours in a structured format. Each region fielded at least eight teams, which played each other on a regional home-and-away basis. Most of the top sides featured Banyana stars. Soweto Ladies (Gauteng), Cape Town Pirates (Western Province), AmaZulu (KwaZulu-Natal) and Classic Chiefs United (Free State) reached the semi-finals. The Gauteng-based side ultimately emerged victorious in the finals, held in Cape Town in May 2002.

Banyana were even busier in 2002. With Shakes Mashaba still serving as technical adviser, they won the inaugural Confederation of Southern African Football Associations (COSAFA) tournament for women in

Zimbabwe, in May, at which twenty-year-old Veronica Phewa shot her way into the record books with an amazing 17-goal blitz, making her the top goal-scorer of the competition. Her incredible run began when she scored eight goals in Banyana's first game, against Botswana, ultimately contributing more than half to South Africa's 14-0 thrashing of their opponents. And there was no stopping her as she went to score four goals in their next game against Mozambique (the full-time score was 13-0 to Banyana Banyana).

South Africa went on to win the inaugural title when they beat hosts Zimbabwe 2-1 in the final.

At the time of writing (September 2002) Banyana were engaged in the qualifiers for the Third Women's African Championships, scheduled for Nigeria in November. With new coach Gregory Mashilo at the helm and former Banyana player Sheryl Botes as his assistant, they were hoping to go through to the final, which would secure them one of two African berths at the senior Women's World Cup to be staged in the People's Republic of China in 2003.

THE BIRTH OF BASETSANA

The national under-19 women's side, a nursery for Banyana, recently campaigned in the African qualifiers for the inaugural Fifa Under-19 Women's World Championships – without much success. Dubbed Basetsana Basetsana, they stumbled at the last hurdle when they were beaten 9-2 on aggregate by Nigeria. But a new mentor, William Seakamela, took over soon afterwards and great things are expected of the side.

Meanwhile Banyana's manager, Fran Hilton-Smith, was appointed to the under-19 championship's technical study group by Fifa, the first time a South African has served at this level. The recognition is well deserved: Hilton-Smith boasts an illustrious playing, coaching and administrative career spanning 35 years.

South African women's soccer looks rosy.

RIGHT *Banyana Banyana's Portia Mtokwane about to leap over a prone Perpetua Nkwocha in the disrupted but historic final.*

CHAPTER 18

AMAGLUG-GLUG: READY FOR THE BIG TIME

South Africa's under-23 soccer stars made only a modest impression at their Olympics debut in Sydney, but have since developed into a closely-knit, disciplined and technically skilled unit.

THE MOOD AT THE SOUTH AFRICAN under-23 national team's hotel in Canberra, their home base for the duration of the 2000 Sydney Olympics, was sombre. AmaGlug-Glug were devastated after losing 2-1 to unheralded Slovenia in their third and final group match.

The South African's lacklustre performance had been in sharp contrast to their confidence-boosting display earlier, when they recorded a stunning victory over the imperious Brazilians – who had been 3-1 winners over Slovenia.

Although AmaGlug-Glug lost to Japan (coached, ironically, by former Bafana Bafana mentor Phillip Troussier) in their first match, they had thought a quarterfinal berth was well within reach. But it was not to be. The first South African soccer side to feature in the Olympics mulled over how close they had come to progressing to the next round. They had valiantly carried the hopes of a nation on their slim shoulders in the months leading up to the Games, and it was a sad end to what had been a promising run.

That run has now been re-started; it continues in earnest, and the youngsters are showing their mettle.

ABOVE *The South African Under-23 team lines up for the national anthem before the match against Japan in Toulon, France, in May 2002. The result – a 3-0 win for the Japanese.*

OPPOSITE *Benni McCarthy beats Slovenia's/Slovakia's Martin Petras to the ball in their match in the Sydney Olympics 2000. The venue: Canberra's Bruce Stadium; the result: defeat for AmaGlug-Glug. In an earlier game, the South Africans had chalked up a stunning 3-0 victory against the regal Brazilians.*

THE FEEDER SCHEME

The team got its name after the South African Football Association secured sponsorship of R3,2 million from petrol company Sasol in 1994 (the baby-word "glug-glug" featured in a prominent series of advertisements). They were to be developed into a closely-knit, disciplined and technically advanced unit.

Safa needed to bolster its development arm, and what better way to do this than to form an under 23-team that would ultimately participate internationally, for top honours, in the All Africa Games and the Olympics?

The side would also serve as feeder to Bafana Bafana, and as the perfect showcase of talent for promising young stars, those who played at club level but saw little international action. Thanks to the scheme, players such as Brian Baloyi, Brandon Silent and Siyabonga

ABOVE *It's mine! – Quinton Fortune (13), one of AmaGlug-Glug's early stars, steals the ball from Namibia's Daniel Motsau.*

Nomvete received exposure, were soon snapped up, and landed lucrative contracts.

The side made their international debut in October 1994 against Ghana, a game which ended in a goalless draw. Three years later Ephraim "Shakes" Mashaba (later coach of the senior side) took over the coaching reins from Mitch D'Avary and began to groom them for, among other events, the 26th Festival International Espoirs, to be held in Toulon, France, in May 1998. They were to become the first African squad to take part in the prestigious tournament.

After scouring the country for talent, Mashaba roped in 150 youngsters and then whittled them down to just 20 for a four-nation tournament held at Soweto's Orlando stadium. Nomvete scored the team's first goal in their opening game, against Zimbabwe, when he netted the ball in the 16th minute. The match ended in a

1-1 draw. After beating Botswana 2-1 in their second game (Nomvete 8th minute and Salmon 25th), they drew 0-0 with Zambia before beating Zimbabwe 2-1 in the final (Steve Lekoelea 50th minute and Daniel Matsau 70th). It had been a fine start to the campaign to put AmaGlug-Glug on the footballing map

The squad then undertook several overseas trips including, most significantly, one to the splendid sports institute in Canberra, Australia, in 1997, benefiting enormously from the technical, nutritional and scientific advice they received at the centre. After Canberra, they went on a similar trip to Germany.

It was a proud moment for the country when "Shakes" Mashaba's lads faced Japan in Sydney in South Africa's first, though unsuccessful, bid for Olympic glory.

Two years later, kicking off their Umbono campaign, they made up for their Olympics failure in dramatic style, delighting the crowd and the country by beating Zimbabwe 3-1 in the final of the Five Nations Cup. Security personnel found it difficult to calm down jubilant fans who hugged, kissed and hoisted the local stars into the air.

But in May 2002, jubilation turned into despair when Italy beat AmaGlug-Glug 4-0 at the Istres stadium in Bardin, France, to eliminate them from the ten-nation Festival International Espoirs. Their 2-1 win over Ireland in the last Group B match was small consolation for a side holding the dubious distinction of conceding more goals – a staggering nine – than any other team at the tournament.

TOWARDS GLORY

To motivate AmaGlug-Glug to win a medal at the 2003 All Africa Games and 2004 Athens Olympics, Sasol have set aside about R2-million as performance bonuses. The company has also allocated more than R34-million for the next three years towards the team's preparation. This is R20-million more than the previous sponsorship. Mashaba has promised a medal in Athens.

But it could be a rocky road – the amiable coach intends grooming an entirely new squad of "unknowns". Mashaba is confident the new crop has what it takes to do better than their predecessors, but they will be a tough act to follow. Most of AmaGlug-Glug's former players, among them Matthew Booth, Benni McCarthy, Quinton Fortune, Aaron Mokoena, Emille Baron, Delron Buckley, Daniel Matsau, Abram Nteo and Stanton Fredericks, became an integral part of South African soccer's *crème de la crème* – arguably the country's best-yet age-group squad.

For the dreams to come true, some niggling problems will have to be addressed – professional clubs who sign up and then bench U-23 players, for example. The practice is frustrating for Mashaba, who sometimes finds himself thinking more about who would turn up than the game plan itself.

Nevertheless there's plenty of promise for the future. A renewed sponsorship and a series of international friendly matches should set the new AmaGlug-Glug well on track to glory.

BELOW *Daniel Matsau chests the ball down as opponents approach.*

CHAPTER 19

SOUTH AFRICANS ON FOREIGN FIELDS

Some of the brightest and best of our soccer stars play abroad, which generates benefits all round. But it also leaves huge gaps in local club line-ups.

THE *KICK-OFF PREMIER SOCCER LEAGUE* guide for the 2001-2002 season has information on 44 South Africans scattered all over the world, from Asia right across to North America. These are exports of South Africa's soccer talent.

And export we have done, and do. In the European leagues, where the emphasis has been on the direct style of play, John Moshoeu's flair came like a breath of fresh air. Moshoeu, who'd made his name on the local scene in the late Eighties, found himself having to answer queries about his intricate dribbling skills. "I get the same question both from fans and from my teammates in Turkey every time I switch on my skills," said Moshoeu in an interview back in 1994.

But back to the main point. A total of 44 players worldwide is not much, you might say, especially if you consider that countries such as Nigeria and Ghana have almost twice that number of professional footballers playing abroad.

Perhaps so, but there are other South African-borns on foreign fields about whom little is known. In reality, the total number is substantially bigger.

Just before the 1998 World Cup in France, players sprang out of nowhere, declaring their South African roots in an effort to get into the squad for the global soccer showpiece. While some, and most notably German-based midfielder Marc Arnold, fell by the wayside, there are those who went on to become Bafana Bafana regulars. The names of goalkeeper Hans Vonk and defender Pierre Issa immediately spring to mind. So, as we've mentioned, the country is even better represented beyond our borders than *Kick-Off* suggests.

OPPOSITE *The twinkle-toed John "Shoes" Moshoeu rounds an opponent in the opening game of the qualifying round for France '98. Moshoeu was based in Turkey for many years.*

EARLY EXPORTS

South African's first exports, nogal during the days of apartheid, were Steven "Kalamazoo" Mokone, Darius Dhlomo and "Hurry Hurry" Johhansen. Kalamazoo, now based in the United States, regularly comes home to Atteridgeville to visit the local soccer scene.

Until just before the 1990s, the ceiling for aspiring soccer stars was to don the famous black-and-gold or black-and-white colours of Kaizer Chiefs and Orlando Pirates respectively. Today, South Africa has a player in almost all the top foreign leagues

Sure, the likes of Kaizer Motaung, Jomo Sono and Ace Ntsoelengoe had stints with overseas clubs in the fairly distant past, but these were more of a rarity. The openings were reserved for the very special talent. Most found homes in American clubs – the US was then seen as a non-soccer country. Very few went to Europe (among them Percy "Chippa" Moloi, who went for trials in England, where soccer is ultra-competitive). Today we have wide representation, even in what is arguably the best club team in the world – Quinton Fortune at Manchester United.

This has had both positive and negative spin-offs for the local game. It has exposed South Africa to the international scene, its skills and its challenges, which has been beneficial to the national team. It has given players an opportunity to develop their individual techniques, which stay with them on their return and raise the standard of the local game. And it has provided income for players and clubs. It needs no mention that Lucas Radebe, appointed captain of Leeds United, is now a millionaire. At one stage he was earning about 10 000 British pounds – more than R100 000 – per week, which amounts to R400 000 per month or R5-million a year.

On the negative side, players left huge gaps in their home line-ups, which, with so many clubs still lacking development structures, meant there were no immediate replacements, and owners

ABOVE Steve Komphela, with future captain Neil Tovey behind him, led Bafana Bafana in the early years. He also played extensively in Turkey.

cial players – top striker Fani Madida late in 1992 to join Turkish side Besiktas; defender Steve Komphela, then captain of the national side, also to Turkey with midfielder John Moshoeu following soon thereafter. Midfielder Ace Khuse also took part in the great trek to Turkey. As if that was not enough, English Premiership side Leeds United scooped defender Lucas Radebe in mid-1994. "It had a very negative effect," says Chiefs boss Kaizer Motaung. "We lost key players at one go and there was no way we could build a winning team immediately." On the other hand, Motaung could not complain that much – Radebe was sold for a then record fee of R1.5-m while the others did not go cheap.

Sundowns also saw top striker Phil "Chippa" Masinga depart for Leeds United, the late Sizwe Motaung also left for Switzerland, striker Mark Williams went to Belgium, and defender Mark Fish joined Italian side Lazio. Doctor Khumalo, who had played in Argentina before, was one of the many foreigners (among them Cape Town Spurs' Shaun Bartlett) who signed up with the new American Major League.

But for some members of the Bafana side that triumphed in the 1996 African Cup of Nations – and especially for Arendse and Helman Mkhalele – that move to the money-spinning leagues was long in coming. It took Arendse over a year after the Nations Cup to realise his dream of a contract with an overseas club. Mkhalele joined the multitudes of his countrymen on the not-so highly-rated Turkish scene.

While the national team was the main showcase for exposing players to foreign clubs, and thus contributed most to the exodus, there was to be another agency at work. In the late 1990s Jomo Sono, renowned as the country's talent spotter supreme, developed a habit of sending his players abroad, among them Kennedy Nagoli, Andrew Rabutla, and Nuro Tualibudine, together with then-unknowns Aaron Mokoena, Maimane Phiri and Lebogang Morula. He dispatches his players overseas, he says, at great cost to his club but "I do what I believe is good for my players". Of course, his club's coffers also swell a little in the process.

Many of Sono's youngsters went abroad on

were forced to go into the market to buy ready-made players.

This happened to Kaizer Chiefs, especially in 1993 and 1994. After winning the league back-to-back in 1991 and 1992, the Amakhosi were to be left high and dry by the departure of cru-

ABOVE *Doctor Khumalo, in training for the World Cup. He played in both Argentina and the American League.*

loan and often returned better players tactically, so much so that they went on to make the national team, and to join the bigger clubs. Godfrey Sapula, now with Orlando Pirates and a regular with Bafana, is a good example.

With time, local player movement to foreign clubs filtered down to include those playing for the junior national sides. In 1997 Benni McCarthy and Junaid Hartley impressed overseas scouts through their exploits for Shakes Mashaba's Under-23 side in both the Africa and World Youth Championships held in Morocco and Malaysia respectively. McCarthy, a top goalscorer in the continental showpiece (where South Africa finished runners-up), went on to join Dutch giants Ajax Amsterdam. He later became a key member of the SA national squad. Hartley, who played only in the world event, moved to France.

CLUB VERSUS COUNTRY

As time went on, though, the South Africans realised that, while it was good for their players to go overseas and mix with the world's best, the experience came at a price. And Bafana paid most of this price. It became increasingly difficult for the technical team to get foreign club players released for national duty – despite Fifa's ruling that enabled national associations to call up their players seven times a year. Some clubs simply refused to toe the line. Whenever an international match was scheduled, there were bound to be doubts about a foreign-based player's ability and availability. In 1995, when Bafana were to meet Argentina in the Nelson Mandela Inauguration Challenge match, Shoes Moshoeu's Turkish club Glencerbirligi took some persuasion before allowing the Bafana midfielder to come home for the match.

ABOVE LEFT *Delron Buckley, who appeared regularly for VfL Bochum in Germany, shoots at goal during the Sydney Olympics.*

ABOVE *Steven Pienaar of Ajax charges forward during a UEFA Champions League match between Ajax and Arsenal played in February 2003.*

RIGHT *Benni McCarthy, presently with Portuguese club Celta de Viga, gets the ball under control in the World Cup 2002 match against Paraguay.*

OPPOSITE CLOCKWISE FROM TOP LEFT *Shaun Bartlett in Charlton Athletic colours; Quinton Fortune, a regular member of the Manchester United squad, in action against Spain at World Cup 2000; Sibusiso Zuma, who played for FC Copenhagen, in a race for the ball with Spain's Mandieta.*

The difficulties were even bigger when it came to England-based footballers: for their work permit to be renewed, they had to have played in 75 percent of their club's matches in the previous season. Aware of their continued unavailability, the clubs often left them out of the team – even when they were available – and thus the players could not fulfil their 75 percent quota. Phil Masinga was a notable victim – at the end of his second season at Leeds United, he failed to have his permit renewed and had to look for a job elsewhere. Luckily he attracted the attention of Swiss side St. Gallen.

The club-versus-country problem was particularly bad in the first years of the millennium, when Trott Moloto was in charge of the national side. One casualty was Mark Fish: his absence from the national side at this time was due to the fact that he was continuously at loggerheads with his club – because of his repeated trips home to play for South Africa.

In need of a solution, the South African Football Association reached a compromise that allowed the likes of Lucas Radebe and Shaun Bartlett to pick and choose their representative matches. This, naturally, did not go down well with most of the local clubs (whose players had no such choice) – they felt that Safa were kowtowing to overseas interests at their expense.

There can be no denying that South African football has made great strides since it has been readmitted to the international arena – progress that is reflected in individual performances, notably those of Lucas Radebe, who captained Leeds, Sibusiso Zuma, voted Denmark's player of the year, and Shaun Bartlett, who scored a goal that was rated the best in an English Premiership that is littered with world class strikers.

And with such stars in the local firmament, there can be no doubt that overseas clubs will continue to recruit our talent.

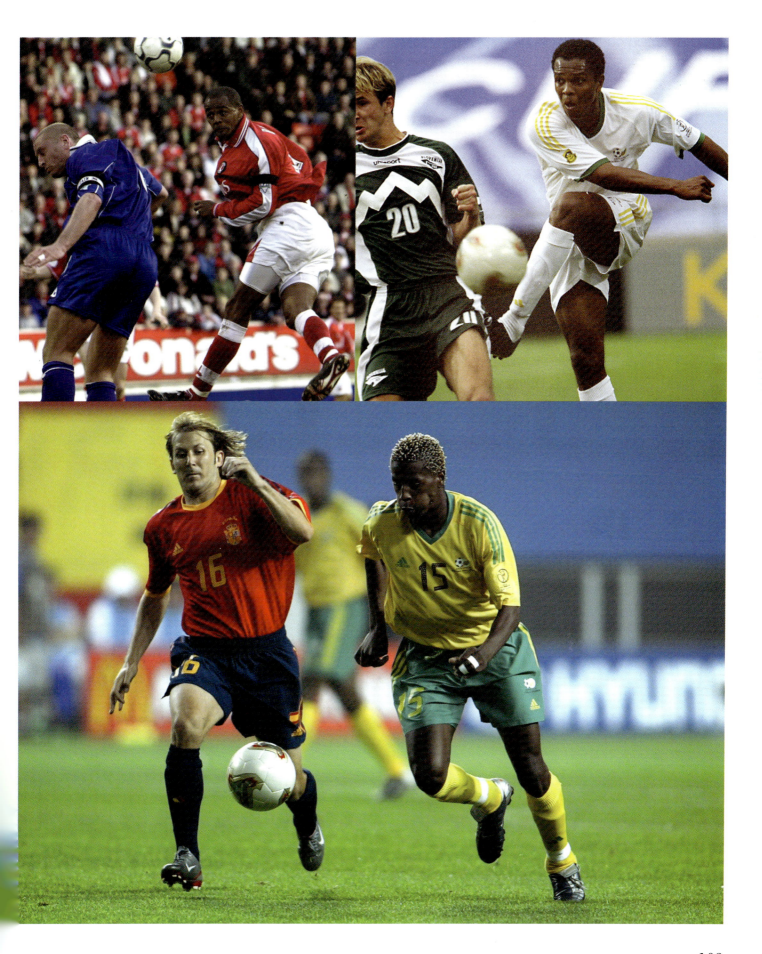

CASTLE PREMIERSHIP

South Africa's principal professional league, launched in 1997 and contested annually by the country's top 18 clubs until the 2001/02 season, when it was reduced to the 16 top clubs. At that point Ria Stars and Free State Stars were omitted and disbanded. The champion qualifies for the CAF Champions League.

1997 Manning Rangers
1998 Sundowns
1999 Sundowns
2000 Sundowns
2001 Orlando Pirates
2002 Santos

AFRICAN CHAMPIONS LEAGUE

Launched in 1964; the following are the results from 1991 to 2002.

1991 Club Africa (Tunisia)
1992 Wydad AC Casablanca (Morocco)
1993 Zamalek (Egypt)
1994 Esperance Tunis (Tunisia)
1995 Orlando Pirates (South Africa)
1996 Zamalek (Egypt)
1997 Raja CA Casablanca (Morocco)
1998 ASEC (Abidjan, Nigeria)
1999 Raja CA Casablanca (Morocco)
2000 Hearts of Oak (Ghana)
2001 Al Ahly (Egypt)
2002 Zamalek (Egypt)

BOBSAVE SUPERBOWL

Knock-out competition: teams from all league divisions. The competition came to an end when FNB withdrew sponsorship after the 2001 event.

1989 Moroka Swallows
1990 Jomo Cosmos
1991 Moroka Swallows
1992 Kaizer Chiefs
1993 Witbank Aces
1994 Vaal Professionals
1995 Cape Town Spurs
1996 Orlando Pirates
1997 No competition
1998 Mamelodi Sundowns
1999 Supersport United
2000 Kaizer Chiefs
2001 Santos

TELKOM CHARITY CUP

Season opener; formerly Iwisa Charity Spectacular

1986 Kaizer Chiefs
1987 Kaizer Chiefs
1988 Kaizer Chiefs
1989 Kaizer Chiefs
1990 Kaizer Chiefs
1991 Cape Town Spurs
1992 Moroka Swallows
1993 Orlando Pirates
1994 Kaizer Chiefs
1995 Orlando Pirates
1996 Kaizer Chiefs
1997 Orlando Pirates
1998 Kaizer Chiefs

1999 Orlando Pirates
2000 Mamelodi Sundowns
2001 Orlando Pirates
2002 Kaizer Chiefs
2003 Kaizer Chiefs

ROTHMANS CUP

Main knock-out competition, Premier Soccer League; replaced by Coca-Cola Cup in 2002

1997 Kaizer Chiefs
1998 Kaizer Chiefs
1999 Mamelodi Sundowns
2000 Ajax Cape Town

COCA-COLA CUP

Knock-out competition, replaced Rothmans Cup in 2002

1992 Amazulu
1993 Umtata Bucks
1994 QwaQwa Stars
1995 Wits University
1996 Umtata Bucks
1997 No competition
1998 No competition
1999 No competition
2000 No competition
2001 Kaizer Chiefs
2002 Jomo Cosmos

BP TOP 8

Contested by the eight clubs at the top of the Castle Premiership. The competition ended in 2002, to be replaced by the SAA Supa 8.

1972 Orlando Pirates
1973 Orlando Pirates
1974 Kaizer Chiefs
1975 Moroka Swallows
1976 Kaizer Chiefs
1977 Kaizer Chiefs
1978 Orlando Pirates
1979 Moroka Swallows
1980 Witbank Black Aces
1981 Kaizer Chiefs
1982 Kaizer Chiefs
1983 Orlando Pirates
1984 Wits University
1985 Kaizer Chiefs
1986 Arcadia
1987 Kaizer Chiefs
1988 Mamelodi Sundowns
1989 Kaizer Chiefs
1990 Mamelodi Sundowns
1991 Kaizer Chiefs
1992 Kaizer Chiefs
1993 Orlando Pirates
1994 Kaizer Chiefs
1995 Wits University
1996 Orlando Pirates
1997 No competition
1998 No competition
1999 No competition
2000 Orlando Pirates
2001 Kaizer Chiefs
2002 Santos

NATIONAL FOOTBALL LEAGUE (NFL)

White clubs only

1970 Durban City
1971 Hellenic
1972 Durban City
1973 Cape Town City
1974 Arcadia Shepherds
1975 Highlands Park
1976 Cape Town City
1977 Highlands Park

NFL CASTLE CUP

Knock-out competition for white clubs only; discontinued end 1977, when clubs joined the NPSL, to launch multi-racial soccer in South Africa

1970 Cape Town City
1971 Cape Town City
1972 Durban United
1973 Highlands Park
1974 Arcadia Shepherds
1975 Highlands Park
1976 Cape Town City
1977 Highlands Park

NATIONAL PROFESSIONAL SOCCER LEAGUE (NPSL)

(Black clubs only until 1978)

The competition ended in 1983, when it was replaced, successively, by the National Soccer League and the Premier Soccer League.'

1971 Orlando Pirates
1972 Zulu Royals (AmaZulu)
1973 Orlando Pirates
1974 Kaizer Chiefs
1975 Orlando Pirates
1976 Orlando Pirates
1977 Kaizer Chiefs
1978 Lusitano
1979 African Wanderers
1980 AmaZulu
1981 Dion Highlands
1982 Hellenic
1983 African Wanderers

Benni McCarthy, Delron Buckley and MacBeth Sibaya in high spirits after McCarthy's second goal against Turkey in the Reunification Cup, Hong Kong, May 23, 2002.

PHOTOGRAPHIC CONTRIBUTORS

Abbreviations: BA = Bailey's Historical Archive; CP = City Press; DM = Drum Magazine; GI = Getty Images; SJ = The Star, Johannesburg; ST = Sunday Times; SW = The Sowetan; TP = Touchline Photo.

b/g = background image; p = page.

Front cover: main picture: ST; cover strip (left to right): ST; Tertius Pickard/TP; SJ; SW; Ben Radford/GI/TP. Back Cover: DM. p1: ST. p2-3: Shaun Botterill/GI/TP. p4-5: Tertius Pickard\TP. p6: TP. p7 (top to bottom): Clive Brunskill/GI/TP; Antonio Muchave/SW; Juda Ngwenya/SW. p9: TP. p10: Gavin Barker/TP. p11 (top to bottom): Gavin Barker/TP; Simon Mathebula/ST; Gavin Barker/TP. p12: TP; TP. p13: (top to bottom): Ben Radford/GI/TP; Ben Radford/GI/TP. p14: TP. p15: Antonio Muchave/SW. p16: DM. p17: BA. p18: BA (b/g); BA. p19 (left to right): BA; DM. p20: BA. p21: BA. p22/23: DM. p24 (top to bottom): ST; (bottom); DM. p25: Associated Press/Denis Farrell/SW (top); ST (below left); DM (below right). p26/27: SW. p28: ST (b/g); Duif du Toit/TP (top); ST (bottom). p29: ST (top) City Press (bottom). p30: SW. p31: ST; ST. p32/33: ST. p34/35: ST (b/g). p34: SJ (left); ST (right). p35: (top to bottom): City Press; SJ; ST. p36: SW. p37: ST. p38-39: DM. p40/41: DM (b/g). p40: DM. p41: DM. p42: City Press. p43: City Press. p44/45: ST (b/g). p44: ST. p45: City Press. p47: TP. p48/49: City Press (b/g). p48: City Press; City Press. p49: City Press. p50-51: Duif du Toit/TP. p52: TP (top); Tertius Pickard/TP (bottom). p53: Tladi Khuele/SW; Tladi Khuele/SW. p54: TP (top); Tsheko Kabasia/SW (bottom). p55: Duif du Toit/TP; Antonio Muchave/SW (bottom) (CHECK: Phil says touchline!, not!). p56: Mark Gleeson/TP. p57: Mark Gleeson/TP. p58: Top: left to right: Mark Gleeson/TP; City Press; Duif du Toit/TP; Tertius Pickard/TP; bottom: Tertius Pickard/TP. p59: TP. p60: ST. p61: Duif du Toit/TP. p62: DM. p63: Duif du Toit/TP. p64: City Press; City Press. p65: City Press (top left); DM (top right); SJ (below). p67: City Press. p68/69: Duif du Toit/TP (b/g). p68: Duif du Toit/TP (top); Shaun Botterill/GI/TP (bottom). p69: Gavin Barker/TP (top); Veli Nhlapo/SW (bottom). p71: SJ. p72: Thembinkosi Dwayisa/SW (top); Duif du Toit/TP (bottom). p73: City Press; City Press. p74: Julani van der Westhuizen / ST. p75: Gary M. Prior/GI/TP. p76/77: City Press (b/g). p76: Thomas Turck/TP (top); Duif du Toit/TP (bottom). p77: Gary Prior/GI/TP. p78: Thomas Turck/TP (top); Tertius Pickard/TP (bottom). p79: TP. p80 City Press. P81: Tertius Pickard/TP. p82/83: TP (b/g). p83: TP. p84: Tertius.Pickard/TP; Tertius Pickard/TP. p86: TP; TP. p87: Jon Hrusa /ST; Jon Hrusa /ST; Jon Hrusa /ST. p88: SW. p89: Gavin Barker/TP. p90: Sefako Mabuya/SW. p91: ST. p92/93 Juda Ngwenya/Reuters (b/g). p92: Duif du Toit/TP (top); Thomas Turck/TP (centre); Stu Forster/GI/TP (bottom). p93: SJ (top); Veli Nhlapo/SW (bottom). p95: Duif du Toit\TP. p96: City Press. p97: Duif du Toit/TP. p98/99: Raymond Preston /ST (b/g). p98: Tertius Pickard/TP. p99: Duif du Toit\TP. p100: Tertius Pickard/TP. p100/101:Tertius Pickard/TP (b/g). p101: Tertius Pickard/TP. p102: SJ. p103: SJ. p104/105: SJ. p106: SJ. p107: Tertius Pickard/TP (left); Duif du Toit/TP (right). p108: Jamie McDonald/GI/TP (top left; TP (bottom). p109: AFP PHOTO:STR (top left); TP (top right); Ben Radford/GI/TP (bottom). p110/111: Tertius Pickard\TP (b/g). p110: TP (top left); Gavin Barker/TP (top right); Duif du Toit/TP. p111: Mark Thompson/GI/TP (bottom); Duif du Toit/TP (top right). p112: TP.